UK AIRSPACE
IS IT SAFE?

UK AIRSPACE
IS IT SAFE?

DAVID OGILVY

Foulis

Haynes
®

A **Foulis** Aviation Book

First published 1989

Published by:
Haynes Publishing Group
Sparkford, Nr. Yeovil, Somerset
BA22 7JJ, England

Haynes Publications Inc.
861 Lawrence Drive, Newbury Park,
California 91320, USA.

British Library Cataloguing in Publication Data
Ogilvy, David *1929–*
    US airspace: is it safe?
    1.   Great Britain. Air traffic. Control. Safety aspects
    I.   Title
    363.1'2472
    ISBN .i.0-85429-726-X

Library of Congress catalog card number 89-84714

Editor: Mansur Darlington
Page layout: Peter Kay
Printed in England by: J.H. Haynes & Co. Ltd

Contents

Introduction

For many years we have been growing in our concern for safety. Whenever the word is used someone, somewhere, seems to leap into action with words to say that we must do something about it. More recently the word 'airspace' has developed equally emotive tentacles and if we place the two alongside each other we have an instant outlet for the press, politicians and others who know the least about it to burst into bouts of exaggeration and drama.

My aim in the pages that follow is to place the subject of safety and airspace in a balanced perspective. We hear so much about the alleged problems of airliners flying too close to other aeroplanes that we could believe the sky to be full, yet the *total* number of aircraft in the UK today is about half the number on the strength of the Royal Air Force in 1918. The civil register lists 12,879 British-owned machines of all kinds and only 685 of these are in use with the commercial air transport sector. We hear about fun fliers in their small aeroplanes being where they should not be and getting in the way of airliners on serious business that is so essential to the nation's economy; yet 87 per cent of seats in airliners operating from UK provincial airports are filled with holidaymakers, seeking their fun in the sun, whilst a very much higher proportion of flights by the lighter aircraft are on essential duties. Not the least of these is club and private flying, which provides a heavy subsidy for the airlines by producing a ready-made and free supply of pilots, without which the commercial operators would be grounded.

Because of the comparatively small number of aeroplanes that exist today, aerodromes, too, are relative rareties. Forty-five years ago there were 21 active airfields in Berkshire alone; today there are three.

Numbers of aeroplanes that aerodromes will accept have diminished steadily, with some air traffic controllers refusing to allow more than three aircraft in their circuit patterns, while when there were large numbers of airfields they were busy: a wartime RAF Elementary Flying Training School operated as many as 110 machines, flying around the local area without the constraints of radio or air traffic control, with pilots – instructors and raw pupils – using their eyes to keep apart from each other, rather than relying on being told through their ears what to do next. I could go on almost endlessly.

If we should have total protection for the commercial air transport sector, as some people argue, would we all agree to adopt a similar principle for the roads?

If so, the private and business motorist would be shunted into the lanes that are not wanted by coaches taking crowds to football matches, or old folk to the seaside, or lorries delivering beer to the pubs. In practice, of course, the reverse applies, with the car driver having access to many places – such as fast lanes on motorways and some town centres – that are out of bounds to the heavy commercial operators. But then those who shout for excessive protection in the air are private motorists who wish to retain their own freedom on the ground.

There are many other aspects to consider. We hear complaints against military aircraft, which according to some should be banned from various areas because they make unwelcome noises or they may be in the way of airliners. Yet these machines have essential duties to perform in the defence of our freedom. Because at home we have lived at relative peace with our neighbours for nearly 45 years, we overlook the importance of having the wherewithal to protect and retain that peace. Numbers of aircraft may be relatively small, but the RAF's Tornado strength alone is more than half the *total* number of airliners of all types in Britain, so occasionally we must expect to hear about them.

Operating his machine and his equipment at high speed and low level, a Service pilot may stray off his intended track; just as inadvertently a private pilot may enter forbidden airspace or an airline pilot may wrongly identify the runway and land on the taxiway; or a controller may give clearance to enter airspace or a runway that is occupied already. No regulations or restrictions will prevent these basic human errors.

In parts of this book I have been very frank and some may say that I have used privilege to unfair advantage as a result of my associations with various aviation organisations. Facts, however, should not be hidden under protective cloaks and only a troubled conscience can be disturbed further by hearing the truth. So I tell the truth here, in the hope that some people may be more cautious before they put forward proposals for changes for political or commercial gain, often in exchange for reduced flight safety for other sections of the aviation community.

Because this truth may be unwelcome, often it is very difficult to find, so here I quote two important facts: there are some heavily-used areas of airspace and there are some very busy airports, but, no doubt surprisingly to many and embarassingly for a few, Heathrow and Gatwick do not feature among them. In the world movements' league, neither is in the top ten, Heathrow taking the UK lead with an unimposing thirteenth place among the centres of commercial air traffic. Gatwick does not feature even in the top 25 in the world listing. In the United States there are individual airports that handle more commercial air transport movements than Heathrow, Gatwick, Stansted, Luton and London City combined. The other point concerns our allegedly crowded airspace: most of it is empty and the only congested spots are caused by the compulsory routing of aircraft into places that their pilots have no desire to go. Quite unnecessarily this reduces safety, but with intelligent planning, there is more than enough room for all.

If our airspace *is* unsafe, whose fault is it? If it isn't, why all the fuss? For the facts, read on . . . .

Author's Acknowledgments

Many people have helped in the preparation of this book. I cannot name them all, not because there are too many to make the list serve a purpose, but because some have asked specifically to remain unknown to the reader. In a couple of cases this is through sheer modesty, but in others it is through fear of reprisal from those with whom they work. In my travels as an aviation consultant I have had opportunities to speak to people in a wide range of posts and positions across the whole aviation spectrum; also I have received letters whose writers are extremely forthright in expressing opinions about things that need to be changed. For whatever reasons such people wish to be unidentified, I have respected their requests. I regret this need for anonymity, especially in a book that espouses the importance of openness, but as you read on you will understand why some contributors wish to keep their names to themselves.

Throughout this book I have endeavoured to assemble the thoughts and opinions of those who have spoken or written and to combine these with my own findings. The results reveal an almost uncanny commonality, for I have received a letter from only one person who wishes everything to be left as it is. So the call for change – not only in airspace planning and use, but in the thinking behind it – rings loud and clear.

Although many must retain the veil of namelessness, some people who have provided information, mainly statistical, can be mentioned and I wish to thank: Dick Barnby (formerly an air traffic controller and watch supervisor at Gatwick Airport, but before that an airline pilot), Ron Campbell (Chairman of the Aircraft Owners and Pilots Association of the UK and Co-ordinator, European Region of International AOPA), Group Captain John Maitland (Officer Commanding the Joint Airmiss Section and Chairman of the Joint Airmiss Working Group, National Air traffic Services), Anne Noonan (Senior Press Officer for the Civil Aviation Authority), John Thorpe (Head of the Safety Promotion Section of the Safety Regulation Group, Civil Aviation Authority), and John Ward (Chairman of the General Aviation Safety Committee and editor of the *Flight Safety Bulletin*). Also I am most grateful to Ian Clark (a former RAF flying instructor and now a solicitor in the Aviation Department of Frere Cholmeley) who has read through the text to advise me on keeping out of trouble.

Where information has come from organisations rather than from individuals I
have mentioned these in the main text, while in some cases, where people have

given permission for their names to be released, I have given direct textual credits for their quotes.

Thanks to the many people who have given their views, as well as those who have provided plain facts, I have presented the situation with greater confidence than would be the case if I had relied solely on my own judgement. Certainly some hard facts must be faced if British aviation is to remain buoyant into the twenty-first century. Many of these relate to safety; and that must concern us all.

David Ogilvy

Chapter 1
Aviation in the UK

THIS CHAPTER is neither critical nor political; any reader who hopes to pitch immediately into pages of hard-hitting attacks on the way in which aviation is organised and controlled may choose to skip it! Later I endeavour to give you some truths in a way that is digestible to the lay reader, yet which will be sufficiently technical for either the professional or the practising enthusiast; but firstly I must try to give a brief but very basic factual description of what UK aviation is all about.

All flying is either civil or military, with a very small overlap that has no effect on the points to be made. Firstly, let us look at the make-up of civil aviation. This is under the control of the Civil Aviation Authority as the regulatory body, but in turn the CAA is responsible to the Department of Transport. The Authority has various departments dealing with flight crew licensing, airworthiness, aerodromes, operations, the legal side and so on. Air traffic control, though, is the one operating angle that is handled on a joint basis with the Ministry of Defence through National Air Traffic Services, which as a combined civil and military organisation, with staff from both sides, exists to co-ordinate the planning and movement of all *controlled* flying in UK airspace. I should mention here, though, that most aircraft in the air are not under any form of air traffic control for the greater part of their flights, even though they may be in radio contact with someone for most of the time; I will explain more about this later. NATS lives in Kingsway, London, while most of the other CAA activities are based on the periphery of Gatwick Airport.

Broadly, civil aviation is divided into two parts:

Commercial air transport
This is the smaller sector in terms of aircraft numbers, movements and numbers of places from which regular flights take place. It comprises the scheduled and charter airline operators, on long-, medium- and short-haul services, together with air taxi companies, which often (wrongly) are excluded from this category, and freight carriers.

The commercial operators are controlled by the CAA through a scheme that requires each company to hold an air operator's certificate appropriate to the type of aircraft and the nature of the work to be carried out. All pilots must hold professional licences; in practice they need instrument ratings and must have type ratings on their licences, valid for the aircraft to be flown. There are differences in the qualification requirements for captains and for first officers, although many of the latter, who are required to hold only Commercial Pilots Licences, hold the full Airline Transport Pilots Licence.

The type of work in this sector varies from the long-haul routes such as those to the United States and the Far East to short hops between the Scottish islands. Aircraft sizes and weights and the operating methods vary equally widely. In the UK most commercial flights are international, for in a year the internal domestic network carries only about the same number of passengers as British Rail transports over mainland Britain on one average working weekday. By far the majority of airline passengers travel to and from Heathrow or Gatwick, while most regional airports carry relatively small numbers. For example, in the month of September 1988, Heathrow moved 3,637,000 people in 28,400 aircraft movements and Gatwick 2,342,600 in 17,600 movements (which was identical with the previous year) while one of the busiest provincials, Birmingham, had an all-time record throughput of 362,278 passengers, or substantially fewer than the number of people who arrive by train at Waterloo between 7 and 10 am each weekday. The least-used international airport in the UK is Prestwick, which despite its enviable weather record on the Ayrshire coast, managed a throughput of only 40,500 people in the month, with a total of just 400 air transport movements. The Prestwick figures show marked reductions compared with the previous year.

There are fewer than 700 aircraft on the UK register that operate in the commercial air transport sector.

General aviation

This is a term imported several years ago from the United States. It covers what in the past we knew as light aviation, together with some other activities such as business aviation in which no money changes hands for the sale of seats. It is by far the largest sector, operating nearly five times the number of aircraft owned by the commercial air transport operators *and* the Services combined.

General aviation stems from the flying clubs and schools, of which there are about 180 in the British Isles. As with the air transport operators, these organisations range from very small units to establishments with fleets and staffs of considerable size. The basic flying qualification is the Private Pilot's Licence, for which there is a syllabus of flying and ground training agreed by the CAA. All schools and clubs are equipped to train people to this standard, but many are geared for the needs of people who seek more advanced achievements in instrument flight, night flying, conversion to multi-engine aircraft, aerobatics and courses to enable suitably experienced pilots to qualify as assistant flying instructors.

Although many people look upon the light side of aviation as a purely fun-flying operation, this is far from the truth. Certainly many private pilots fly purely for their own personal pleasure in the same way as people drive cars or sail yachts for enjoyment, but without the club and private flying movement the commercial air transport sector would collapse through a lack of new pilots. Each year hundreds of young people learn to fly at their own – considerable – expense and continue to gain flying experience by what is known as the 'self-improver' route until they are ready to take the relevant tests and examinations for their professional licences. Many of these individuals abandon life's luxuries so that they can afford to achieve their ambitions. This arrangement ensures a constant (if still inadequate) supply of new junior officers for the airlines, which otherwise would need to spend many millions of pounds each year on sponsored pilot training schemes. Certainly some more forward-thinking operators are placing selected students through the professional training schools, but the numbers fall seriously short of known requirements, so, in practice, from their own pockets many private pilots are providing substantial subsidies for the air transport industry. This cuts the cost of your holiday journeys.

General aviation covers a very wide field; activities under this broad heading include ambulance flights, mercy missions on which human organs are rushed to people in need, crop spraying and dusting, police, motorway and pollution patrols, air survey and aerial photography, business flying and, of course, private and club flying.

There are 10,059 aircraft on the UK register that fall within the GA category. The interests of their owners and operators are handled mainly by the Aircraft Owners and Pilots Association (AOPA) and the Popular Flying Association (PFA).

Service aviation

The Royal Air Force operates the largest fleet of military aircraft in the UK, but the Royal Navy and the British Army have substantial numbers on their inventories. Also, the United States Air Force has several squadrons based in Britain. In this short explanation I shall group their activities together, as there are many factors that are common to all the Services.

An important point here is that military flying covers a much wider range of activities than is the case with civil aviation. There are light single-engine aircraft (piston and jet) used for basic pilot training, aircraft on communications work, helicopters on numerous tasks, fast-flying front-line machines, most of which must operate (and the crews for which must train for operations) at low level, and heavier types used for transport, flight refuelling and maritime patrol duties, some of which operate in manners not dissimilar to civil airliners. So the needs of the Services are many and varied.

The numerical strengths of the various Services are not revealed publicly, but probably there are about 1500 military aircraft based in the UK – or roughly twice as many as the number of commercial air transport aircraft.

Airports, aerodromes and airfields

These fall into several categories. As with all aviation, some are civil and others are operated by the Services. A few are available for both and are known as 'joint user' airfields. Strictly speaking, airports and aerodromes are civil and airfields are military, although these terms are spread fairly loosely.

Any airport used for commercial air traffic must be licensed by the CAA. Licences come in various categories and are related to the size of aircraft that may be operated commercially. Also, any aerodrome used for flying training for the purpose of a person gaining a licence, or a rating on a licence, must be licensed. The requirements vary considerably, but relate to the provision of adequate crash/rescue facilities, markings of runways, obstruction-free approaches and other factors affecting safety. Civil Air Publication (CAP) 168 – The Licensing of Aerodromes gives all details including, for example, the requirement for a fire tender to be able to travel from its stabling point to the runway threshold in 2 minutes.

For a non-commercial operation, whether a private pilot flying for pleasure, a farmer using a light aeroplane to inspect his crops or an air transport operator taking a machine to or from a maintenance base for servicing, there is no requirement to use a licensed aerodrome. There are 136 licensed civil aerodromes and probably about three hundred private airstrips throughout the British Isles. As the strips are not licensed and many are for the personal use of their owners, there is no central record and the exact number is not known.

(Sometimes we read in the paper that an aeroplane was landing, for instance, on runway 09 Left at Heathrow, so perhaps a few words here may help. This is not the *number* of the runway, ie it is not number nine, but refers to the first two figures of the magnetic heading. Therefore an easterly direction (090 degrees) would be 09. The opposite end of the same runway, heading to the west (270 degrees) would be 27. Heathrow has two parallel runways running approximately east-west, designated 09L and 09R; heading in the opposite direction, from the other end, the same runways become 27R and 27L respectively. The standby runway in a broadly north-east/south-west direction, ie 050 degrees and 230 degrees, is known as 05/23.)

Whether an aerodrome is licensed is not necessarily a function of its size or a measure of the scope of its facilities, but is based on the type of operations carried out. For example, the well-known British Aerospace flight test centre at Bristol (Filton), with a runway 2492 metres in length (longer than the secondary runway at Heathrow), was the place from which the British Concorde made its first flight, but had no need to be – and was not – licensed. Yet Netherthorpe, near Worksop, where the longer of two grass runways has a length of 450 metres, qualifies for – and holds – a licence. I mention this to remove any possibility of fear that an unlicensed aerodrome must be unsafe.

Seven UK airports – Heathrow, Gatwick, Stansted, Prestwick, Glasgow, Edinburgh and Aberdeen – are owned by BAA plc (formerly the British Airports Authority) and a few around Northern Scotland and the islands are owned by the CAA. Most provincial airports are in the hands of local authorities, for although theoretically they were compulsorily privatised relatively recently, in most cases all the shares have been issued to their original owners. Some aerodromes – in the main the smaller ones – are in genuine private ownership. Airfields operated by the flying Services are owned by the Ministry of Defence. There is a substantial increase in the numbers of owners who keep their aircraft at private strips, but a marked reduction in the number of both licensed and military aerodromes, compared with previous years.

The representative organisation for airport and aerodrome operators is the Aerodrome Owners Association (AOA).

Airspace

Because this word appears in the title of the book, you may wonder why it earns just a few paragraphs here. The reason is that all aircraft must operate in some form of airspace and, before we go into action in the following chapters, a few words on the subject may be helpful.

The pattern of airspace over the UK is complicated and there is no need for a detailed understanding of its whys and wherefores. All the usable sky falls into one category or another, however, and, in broad terms, this is either controlled or uncontrolled. Although there is no formal statutory meaning to the word 'regulated' when referring to airspace, it is used frequently as an easy way in which to define various areas and I will take the liberty of using this unofficial term at suitable points throughout the book. So we have two basic categories:

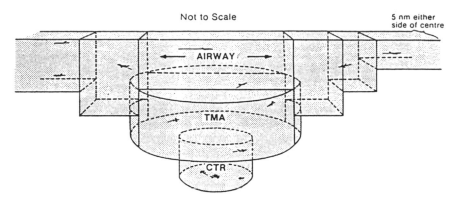

This is a 3D example of how the airspace around a typical group of airports is regimented. The controlled airspace includes a control zone, a terminal manoeuvring area, and airways.

Unregulated: This is the air in which there is no formal control over a pilot's actions. Over the UK it is divided into two Flight Information Regions and usually is described as the 'open FIR'. A pilot may be in radio contact with a control centre and receiving any one of a number of levels of service, but the responsibility for remaining clear of other aircraft rests with him. This is based on the requirement for a pilot to maintain a thorough lookout and to operate on the 'see-and-avoid' principle. In this open airspace, in conditions of poor visibility a pilot is expected to achieve vertical separation from other aircraft that may be on different headings by flying at a quadrantal height, which ensures that an aeroplane flying in, say, a north-easterly direction will have a vertical distance of not less than 1000 feet from a machine flying the opposite way.

Regulated: This takes many forms; it may be a control zone around a major airport such as Heathrow, or a terminal manoeuvring area, which is a larger area around one or more major centres of activity. The London Terminal Area, for example, embraces Heathrow, Gatwick, Stansted, Luton and London City and covers a vast amount of south-east England. Between the areas of protected airspace surrounding the major airports are broad bands of restricted air known as airways. A control zone starts from the surface, while a terminal area or airway has some free air beneath it. Although there are various exceptions, in the main most general aviation aircraft are restricted to that free airspace.

Other parts of the sky that have marked restrictions on their use include military training areas, danger areas (usually surrounding firing ranges), areas of intense aerial activity, parachute jumping zones and areas immediately surrounding all licensed aerodromes, known as aerodrome traffic zones. Not all these are active at all times and a pilot may need to spend some effort researching an intended route to discover those through which he may fly, those which he may penetrate by calling on the radio for a crossing service and those around which he must plan a detour.

In recent years the amounts of regulated airspace have increased substantially and these have caused considerable complications that will be aired later in the book.

Information

14 A pilot is required to retain in his head certain basic general information such as

the Rules of the Air, so that he knows what action to take if he sees another aircraft that may lead to a possible conflict, the height at which he may fly over a built-up area and the weather minima in which his licence or rating on his licence entitles him to operate. For detailed knowledge of the many variables, however, there is a vast volume, the *Aeronautical Information Publication (AIP)*, colloquially known as the Air Pilot which is amended regularly. Only reasonably permanent information finds its way into this great tome and this takes time to filter through the system, so an important information source is the Notam (which started life as a *Not*ice to *Air*men) and this comes in two main forms: permanent and temporary. The first serves as early warning for details that eventually will find their ways into the Air Pilot, whilst the latter gives prior notice of military exercises, flying displays, temporary runway closures, unserviceability of radio navigational aids and other points of pertinence. Administrative matters are contained in a separate series of CAA sheets known as Aeronautical Information Circulars (AICs). The range of safety-related documents includes General Aviation Safety Information Leaflets, Air Accident Investigation Branch Bulletins, General Aviation Safety Sense, Analyses of Airmisses in the UK, Flight Safety Bulletin and others. Also there are numerous more permanent Civil Air Publications and each of these carries a CAP number (eg CAP 168: The Licensing of Aerodromes, already mentioned).

In general, there is no shortage of available information, but it takes time to digest and put into practical use.

Representation

The Civil Aviation Authority is the UK regulatory body, but it relies largely on information and inputs from numerous representative sources and has certain established consultative processes with the various sectors. There are dozens of organisations with their own parts to play or axes to grind and I will not give a long catalogue of them all, but you will understand the wide range of needs and interests when I mention the Aerodrome Owners Association, the Aircraft Owners and Pilots Association, the Business Aircraft Users Association, the British Airline Pilots Association, the Flying Farmers Association, the Guild of Air Pilots and Air Navigators, the British Microlight Aircraft Association, the British Gliding Association, the Popular Flying Association, the Guild of Air Traffic Control Officers, the British Hang-Gliding Association . . . I could go on. Not surprisingly there are frequent conflicts of opinion and these are aired energetically at the relevant national meetings of official bodies such as the Standing Advisory Committee on Pilot Licensing and the National Air Traffic Management Advisory Committee. Safety is taken seriously in all quarters through the Flight Safety Committee (which is airline orientated) and the General Aviation Safety Committee, which handles the subject for other airspace users.

These are permanent bodies, but perhaps a new proposal from one quarter of aviation may create problems for others and may require considerable effort to resolve. In such a circumstance, a small working group may be established and those with direct interests in the specific subject are able to reach solutions – often in compromise form – by devoting one or more meetings exclusively to that task.

I promised that this explanation would be brief and here I have not failed you. However, if these facts have been a bit uninspiring I hope that the following chapters will provoke a little more mental activity!

Chapter 2
What is Safety?
And Who Cares?

APPARENTLY we are all very worried about the safety of the various activities that go on in the skies above us. I use the word 'apparently' because I am not convinced that in general we really care so very much about safety. Not so long ago, indisputable statistics revealed that on a mile-by-mile basis we are 25 times more likely to be killed travelling in a car than we are if we take our journeys in a train; but did we all abandon the known trauma of the roads and transfer our bodies to the safety of the rails?

Firstly let us look at what safety is. Like worry, it is an attitude of mind. A dictionary definition of safe is 'free from danger' and for worry we read 'to be unduly anxious; to fret'. So when we put the two words together we have the ready-made recipe for alarm. Mix-in some drama from the media and periodical pressure from the politicians; then, without great difficulty, we are convinced that every airliner is about to hit another or that some irresponsible pleasure pilot in his light aeroplane is flying in the path of a machine loaded with fare-paying passengers.

To place the picture the right way up we need to examine a few facts, by comparing what happens today with the scale of flying activities in the past, for we have been led into believing that there are far more aircraft flying now than ever before and that we have insufficient space in the air to accommodate them. Many organisations and individuals must share the blame for spreading so much false information and in a later chapter I take these to task for their politically-motivated actions; however, let us begin our search by placing both feet firmly on the ground.

Firstly, in earlier years, the skies of Britain saw far more aircraft and far more flying than we see now or are likely to see ever again. By the end of the First World War in 1918 the Royal Air Force had on strength more than 22,000 aeroplanes. In the Second World War more than 20,000 Spitfires alone were built. Today we have on the UK civil register about 12,900 aircraft of all kinds. Between them the Services account roughly for a further 1500, making a grand total of about 14,400 machines including balloons and microlights. Of these, fewer than 700 (about 5%) are operated by the commercial air transport sector; or, put in perspective, if all the airliners, big and small, could be serviceable at one time and put into the air together, the result would be a smaller gaggle than the number of RAF aircraft that went on some *single* bombing raids from Britain during the Second World War. There was no controlled airspace, the raids took place at night, the aircraft were concentrated in a relatively small area and for most of the time their lights were shielded or extinguished and there was radio silence. Captains of aircraft were just that, and were responsible for the safety of their own aircraft and crews.

Today, when we hear some controllers enforcing arbitrary restrictions on the number of aircraft flying round their aerodrome circuits, we must wonder who is protecting whom and from what. In practice, they could be working themselves out of jobs, for the busiest aerodromes in the history of aviation were those at which there was no form of air traffic control. Certainly there is a limit to the number of machines that can be handled effectively if radio calls are to be made at each position, but good traditional airmanship, based on the see-and-avoid principle, enabled hordes of aircraft to operate from the aerodromes that were scattered throughout Britain in the Second World War. Already I have mentioned that in 1945 there were 21 active aerodromes in Berkshire compared with three today, but this picture of current inactivity applies almost everywhere.

CAP 481 (United Kingdom Aerodrome Index, dated February 1988) lists no fewer than 261 former *civil* aerodromes in the UK that have ceased operations. Although some of these date back to the early days of flight, others were in use more recently: among them were Ashford (Lympne), Balado Bridge, Beaulieu, Belfast (Nutt's Corner), Bitteswell, Bristol (Whitchurch), Broxbourne, Cardiff (Pengam Moors), Chilbolton, Christchurch, Coventry (Ansty), Cowes (Somerton), Hamble, Hastings (Pebsham), Husbands Bosworth, Jurby, Leicester (Desford and Rearsby), Loughborough, Portsmouth, Pwllheli (Broom Hall), Ramsgate, Reading (Woodley), Ryde (Isle of Wight), Tarrant Rushton, Weston Super Mare and Wolverhampton. Since the official list was published, Aylesbury (Thame) has joined the growing band of aerodromes no longer available for use. Although a few of these sites have been replaced by others in their respective neighbourhoods, in most cases the areas concerned have been stripped of flying facilities and the net loss of both civil and military airfields in the past 30 years amounts to a very substantial figure.

Not only should we be concerned here with the number of aerodromes, but the amount of activity that occurred at most of them. Whilst some operational stations were exceptionally busy at peak times – I remember watching 70 Mustangs of the (then) United States Army Air Corps joining-up in six minutes to make a protective fighter formation to accompany B-17 Fortresses on a daylight bombing mission – the training bases could claim the most consistent levels of heavy traffic. An elementary flying training school could have as many as 110 machines on strength, but more·of that later.

You may feel that a comparison between the enforced pressures of activity in wartime and today's situation is unjustified, for when a nation is at full strength fighting for its own survival, greater levels of risk must be acceptable. Let us look, then, at the situation as some of us faced it in the fifties, at which time we were several years into the period of peace that we continue to enjoy.

At that time there were hundreds of active aerodromes in the British Isles. Although many of these came into existence because of the need to operate large numbers of military aircraft in defence of the nation during the Second World War, this was not the only reason for the wide distribution of airfields over the UK; indeed, many of them came to life in the thirties and some were too small to be of serious operational use during the war. So, for a variety of reasons, in the fifties we had the use of far more places from, and to, which to fly than we have 17 now. Even in post-war Britain, the Services operated many more airfields than they need in the eighties for, all over the UK, the Royal Air Force had Auxiliary Squadrons with front line fighters such as Meteors and Vampires; and Reserve Flying Schools with Tiger Moths and, later, Chipmunks. The Royal Navy, too, had its geographically spread Reserve Units with Sea Furies and Fireflies. Then there were the smaller 'friendly fields' that formed such an important part of the overall pattern of club and private flying.

Let us take a brief look at the south-east coast. After reading the list of closures earlier in this Chapter we find ourselves left with just Shoreham, Goodwood and once again Lydd as the only currently active places. But when Ramsgate, Lympne, Hastings, Christchurch and Portsmouth were generating civil traffic, this was interspersed with activity from military airfields such as Lee-on-Solent, Thorney Island, Tangmere and Ford. If anyone feels that there were no potential problems of conflict because aircraft speeds were generally much more comparable, let us not forget that Moths (all without radio) and Meteors mixed it regularly and no one had acquired the over-defensive habit of complaining that too may aeroplanes were getting in each others' way. There were aircraft and aerodromes almost everywhere and everyone lived together quite happily. A private pilot plodding along the coast in his Auster or Messenger thought nothing (and doubtless enjoyed) the sight of a flight of Fireflies crossing his bows in formation or meeting a Vampire going round the coast in the other direction with only a few hundred feet separation, or a fully laden DC-3 or Heron climbing out of Hurn *en route* to Jersey in the early days of the fun-in-the-sun trips that seem to be among the main causes of problems with airspace today.

So why now do we make so much fuss whenever two aeroplanes come within sight of each other? Safety is important and we must take a very serious view of deliberately dangerous practices, but the whole subject seems to have degenerated into one in which disputes and disagreements come to the fore. Someone always is striving to protect his position (or possibly his pension) on a piecemeal basis rather than aviation settling down to live with itself. The important message here is that we are becoming increasingly over-protective in almost every sphere of activity and when this extends to aviation, which it is doing, then we become excessively restricted and counter-productive.

All this revolves around attitude of mind. When one aerodrome in the Midlands imposed a limit of three aircraft in its ATZ at any one time, several experienced pilots who operated from there made some very derogatory remarks about this arbitrary and unnecessary restriction; yet a few years later a new generation of private pilots had been brought up in this over-constrained environment and were led into thinking from the start that four aeroplanes in the circuit must create a hazard. That attitude has developed throughout the airspace and now we hear a fuss whenever two aircraft are in sight of each other.

What we need is progress. In itself the gradual introduction of VHF radio into light aircraft was a sensible if inevitable move, but unfortunately, through misuse, it has become a tool of constraint. In many cases its intended purpose has become misunderstood. Both pilots and controllers have become accustomed to relying on what comes to their ears rather than basing their decisions on what they can see. As evidence of this backward move, one private pilot who rang a GA aerodrome for permission to land was told that as air traffic would not be open there would be no radio communications and that he should join visually. In reply he said that if no one could tell him which way to land he would not be coming.

Moving from the South Coast let us have a look at a typical aerodrome in the Midlands that once saw intensive activity: Derby (Burnaston). After many years of total closure it was reopened recently as a single strip with a resident flying club and a few private owners. Now, however, it may be closed again permanently – to make way for a Japanese car factory. Thirty-five or so years ago it was an active omni-directional airfield that housed a Royal Air Force Reserve Flying School, the Derby Aero Club and several private aircraft. The Service unit operated about 35 aircraft. This was not an exception, but was typical of aerodromes spread over the British Isles which, for obvious reasons, were near to centres of population. London had similar places around it on all sides.

Most people felt then that Burnaston was a busy airfield, but ten years or so before that it had been even busier; 108 Magisters were based there and each morning 70–75 of these took off to fill the local airspace on circuits, cross-countries, stalling, spinning, aerobatics and other aerial activities essential to the training of Service pilots. There was no radio, no air traffic control and regularly about twenty of the aircraft were in the circuit area going about their business with neither fear nor fuss. First solos were slotted into this without difficulty. This situation was repeated at dozens of other places all over Britain. Since then, progressively, we have adjusted our minds to living with fewer aircraft, fewer aerodromes and virtually empty airspace almost everywhere. Yet we pretend that we are short of it – and even short of radio frequencies to enable us to spend our lives telling each other where we are; but perhaps this is essential because there are so few of us and we are unlikely to be close enough to see each other.

Perhaps it was the virtual demise of the Royal Air Force Volunteer Reserve, the Royal Auxiliary Air Force and the Royal Naval Volunteer Reserve units that brought aviation activity down to a very low base; perhaps also the very gradual increase since that trough has caused newcomers to the scene to feel that the airspace is more fully occupied than it has been. In the early fifties, whether watching from the ground or in the air, it was usual to see several aircraft in flight almost anywhere and at almost any time. Service and civil pilots – private and professional – used their eyes and geared their brains to those eyes; because almost every pilot came fairly close to several others on almost every day, what now might be filed as an airmiss would not have qualified even as worthwhile bar talk.

No one in his senses wishes to expose himself or anyone else to unreasonable levels of risk, but again the meaning of 'unreasonable' must be related to attitude and outlook. When we kill each other at the rate of about 16 people every day on the roads, sometimes with juggernauts careering out of control into the fronts of private houses, why have we become so paranoid about the need for total protection when we are in the air? The logical, if impracticable, solution to the first problem would be to ban all vehicles from all roads, or to keep mere private cars away from the public transport operators taking coach-loads on the serious business of seaside outings or football matches, yet because drivers, passengers, cyclists and pedestrians die daily, the topic has faded from the headlines and we accept this mass destruction of human life as a part of the pattern of modern existence. Only because – fortunately – incidents and serious accidents to aircraft are relative rarities do we engage ourselves in so much discussion on the subject. So do we *really* care about our own safety? Is the fear factor real or is it – like AIDS – a fear of a developing disease that no one seems to be able to check?

Every activity carries a risk element. If we pursue the argument to an irrational 19 conclusion we will return to the old adage that more people die in bed than anywhere else, so would we be safer not to retire to sleep at the end of the day? Of course this is not a reasonable or a responsible proposal, but it does help to place into perspective our possibly misguided views on safety.

If there is a problem – and almost certainly it is perceived rather than real – it has been compounded beyond all reasonable proportions by the media. Not long ago one newspaper reported that two airliners came within half a mile of each other while another journal quoted the same 'incident' as a horizontal separation of 4 miles. Later the CAA issued a press release stating, quite accurately, that there had been no incident at all! Whilst there are problems in obtaining accurate information – especially at the short notice needed by a daily publication – the fact that in this and in most other reported cases someone is wrong must cause unnecessary tensions and these have run-on effects in many quarters.

To return to our senses, do we all need some shock treatment or can we achieve success through the educational drip-feed system? However we get there, remember this: on the road we drive within a few feet of other vehicles going in the opposite direction at legitimate closing speeds of up to 140 mph. Head-on impact in such a case would be as terminal to life as would mid-air contact at considerably higher speeds, yet we live in the midst of such a hazardous situation on the road with hardly a moan. So let us be thankful for the emptiness of our skies and live happily in the relative tranquillity that such open spaces offer. In short, we should stop moaning and remember that there are only half the number of aeroplanes in Britain today that there were in 1918.

Constantly we are told that airspace in the south-east is heavily congested, but many people wonder how this can be when there is so relatively little flying and there are so few aerodromes compared with earlier years. The answer lies in the piecemeal planning – if planning is not too polite a word – that has led to our present airspace layout. Certainly, readers living under approach or climb-out paths in line with runways at Heathrow and Gatwick may wish to invite me to see and hear what they suffer, but I know the situation as my sister lives in just such a place. For most of us in most places, however, aeroplanes are relative rarities. I have carried out checks in several appropriate spots and I have been surprised to find even less aerial activity than I had expected. Along the south coast near the Kent/Sussex border, which was part of the Cross-Channel Special Rules Area (and therefore considered to hold enough air traffic to qualify as a form of restricted airspace) I was outdoors on a cycling holiday for virtually a whole week. The weather was fine and, on average, I saw fewer than six aircraft in total on each day. My home is under a part of the London Terminal Area, which is banned to most general aviation aircraft because allegedly it is full of commercial air traffic. At no time in the past year have I seen or heard more than ten airliners in any one day. During a recent week in Yorkshire I saw more aircraft than I have seen in a similar time in the London area.

I close this chapter with a suggestion. Have a notepad with you and make a mark each time you see or hear an aeroplane. Unless you are on the direct approach to Heathrow or Gatwick or under the circuit pattern of an airfield such as Wycombe Air Park or Biggin Hill, or beneath one of the narrow funnels into which general aviation traffic is squeezed quite unnecessarily, you will surprise yourself at the few occasions on which you will unite pencil and paper. So where, oh where are all these aircraft that are causing so much concern, and why do we not see them wherever we happen to be? Is it the long eerie silence that causes us to worry?

Chapter 3
Comparative Safety

IF THE WORD safety is to have any meaning it must be used in a comparative context. Unfortunately, however, in seeking direct relationships between the safety values in the four travel modes – road, rail, sea and air – we begin by finding that most available information is not provided on a comparable basis. As an example, whilst the claim that in terms of travelling distances we are 25 times more likely to be killed in a car than in a train may well be supportable, when we study the statistics produced by the Royal Society for the Prevention of Accidents (RoSPA) we find a different answer. Here the table shows, for each billion passenger kilometres travelled, that over a period of ten years the death rate was 0.3 by rail or air and 5.9 in a car. This shows a factor of 19.5 between car and air or rail; or it does so until we read the very small print, which states that the figure for air travel excludes aircraft crew and covers only revenue-paying passengers, while the rail total includes passengers *and* staff involved in all train accidents. It is well known that railway personnel suffer from accidents in marshalling yards and in other operating spheres, but if we wish to make worthwhile comparisons we need information on a more easily-identifiable basis.

In practice, the RoSPA figures do not enable us to extract the precise detail that would provide clear-cut comparisons, but the information is sufficient to show clearly the order of safety in life survival terms. Motorcycles head the accident list at 156 deaths per billion passenger kilometres, or 500 times greater than the figure for travel by air. Perhaps most surprisingly – and here in each case the figures are based on passengers travelling in UK-registered ships and aircraft respectively – the death rate at sea is 1.8 per billion passenger kilometres, or 6 times greater than the rate for people flying in airliners. Such statistics could be distorted, of course, by one major disaster that swamped the totals for the ten-year period, but this is not so; passengers were killed at sea in each of the years for which information is provided, while in the case of air travel no passengers were killed in 1981, 1982, 1983, 1984 or 1986, which was the final year of the survey.

If we extend the detail to include serious injuries, air travel heads the list in safety terms, with fewer than 0.1 people badly hurt for a billion passenger kilometres covered, while the car figure is 22, or substantially more than 200 times worse. The figure for motorcyclists is 3,059, but that for serious injuries at sea cannot be isolated, as the quoted average of 39.7 covers four years only and includes all injuries regardless of whether they were serious or minor.*

All these figures in isolation, although not entirely comparable, make interesting and useful study, for apart from offering comfort in the extreme levels of safety of both air and rail travel, they enable us to place in perspective the likelihood of coming to any form of harm when travelling in any of the four modes, with road figures sub-divided into three sections. By extraction from published information we find:

Mode	*Order of likelihood of* Death	Serious injury
Motorcycle	1	1
Car	2	2
Coach or bus	3	3
Sea	4	4*
Air	5	6
Rail	6	5

* Qualified as in paragraph above

So, in brief, although we are more likely to be killed in an aeroplane than on a train, with no precisely comparable figures available, we are more likely to be injured in a train than in an aeroplane. Bearing in mind the different styles of operation of the two modes, this is an easily predictable and therefore not surprising statistic; but the most significant news of all is that air and rail travel are so much safer than any of the other methods that I could stop at this point and answer the question in the title of this book with an unqualified 'yes'! I will not release you from bondage at this early stage, however, and I intend to give you some more convincing facts of life – with stress on 'life', or the extent to which we place our values on it.

The figures that I have quoted so far in this chapter have been geared as closely as possible to direct comparisons, but sometimes bare facts in themselves, whilst not measurable in relation to each other except in total terms, bring home the facts that surround us so inescapably. Information emerges from many sources, and figures for 1985 (the latest year for which *all* details are available) reveal some surprises. Not so surprising, though, is the perpetually top-of-the-list figure for accidents involving road transport which accounted for 5,583 deaths. This was followed by 4,643 fatalities through accidental falls. The lowest figure for all accidental deaths went to a heading known as air/space transport, with 50 deaths registered in the year, with rail claiming 101 lives. Remember though, the significance of the word 'all' in this context, for these totals include all fatal accidents relating to aircraft and rail operations. Comparably 82 people died in the year in connection with shipping services, while drownings that were not transport-related were 314; incidentally, more people drown in cars than in boats. These totals, relating to Great Britain as a whole, are extracted from tables prepared for the Office of Population Censuses and Surveys in London and the General Register Office in Edinburgh.

Whilst these all-embracing figures are encouraging for both the air and rail traveller, a few comments about the ways in which these transport modes differ in their methods of operating – and the numbers of these operations—may be significant. Firstly, British Rail operates 16,000 trains and carries more than

2,000,000 people on each working weekday, growing at a current rate of 5 per cent annually. It is impossible to assess the total number of train movements in stop/start terms, which on a small scale are comparable with airport arrivals and departures. I must stress the comparison of scale, because just as take-off and landing are the times at which an aeroplane is operating at its greatest level of risk, so in a minor way each time a train stops at or pulls out of a station, the consequences of technical failure and the opportunities for human error are at their peak. Possibly the potential seriousness of such error may be smaller at this juncture than it is, for example, when a train driver ignores a signal whilst travelling at high speed, but at station stops the number of people who are in positions to cause accidents are at their greatest, because many passengers endeavour to board and alight when trains are moving. Fortunately many recent carriage designs have incorporated sliding instead of slam doors and, as more of these are introduced, this alone is likely to show a progressive decrease in the numbers of self-inflicted injuries. There is no comparable situation in air travel terms, which helps to reduce the number of injuries among airline passengers.

I mention this because here the two modes reunite in problem terms. In 1987 a summary of accidents produced by the Chief Inspecting Officer of Railways revealed a series of cases in which drivers had failed to accept that rules are rules, mainly in connection with signals. Most of the older drivers, many of whom had retired recently, had served in the Forces and had learned that to disobey orders could lead to severe disciplinary action, the thought of which deterred them from stepping too far out of line. Also, discipline at home and in schools had been at high levels. Many newer and younger members of train crews had not experienced either the meaning of rigid rules or the penalties for defying them, and this was revealed in a number of cases in which trains came to grief. The main point, though, is that in the same month a report emerged from New Zealand expressing similar findings in the flying world and for similar reasons: as a result, there had been instances of airline pilots looking upon instructions more as guidelines to be considered than as orders to be obeyed. I do not intend this as a subjective criticism brought about by a generation gap, but clearly this factor is one that plays a key role with all activities in which actions of individuals can affect the safety of large numbers of other people. Certainly it is one that needs to be studied more fully than appears to have been the case so far.

Returning to numbers, commercial air transport movements at the six busiest UK airports, which between them account for probably 90 per cent of all genuine airline traffic, amounted to an average of about 63,400 for each of the middle six months of 1988, while terminal passengers averaged approximately 6,500,000 during the same half-yearly period. This gives a very rough figure of slightly more than 100 passengers per aircraft, with 216,000 passengers and 2,100 aircraft movements a day. An interesting comparison between travel modes is that the figure for rail produces about 120 people on each train. Unfortunately it is impossible from available information to extract typical load factors, for train capacities – from single railcars to inter-city expresses with 12 or more coaches – cover wide ranges and the variation in aircraft seating between small regional and long-haul international airliners is even greater.

Clearly, because an air accident is such a rare occurrence, when one happens the average figures are of minor significance, for one example in a year could relate to a machine at either end of the size and capacity range or to any type in between, so yearly numbers are of no value; even ten-year averages can be distorted by one unfortunate fatal accident. This is not so likely, though, in figures for rail, where 23 a larger number of relatively minor incidents can provide more meaningful information. In an extreme case in which there were no air transport accidents for ten years and then in one year two large aircraft came to grief, the figures for that year would look atrocious, but would mean absolutely nothing in terms of safety trends. So it is important not to sound mental alarm bells when just one aeroplane fails to deliver its passengers safely to its destination; an accident *can* happen anywhere and at any time – and no action on anyone's part will prevent that as a possibility – but for an airliner the *likelihood* is much less than on any other form of transport.

There are, perhaps, two significant points here. Firstly, for about one-eighth the number of movements and passengers, the air transport industry retains all the airspace shown in the airspace diagram for 1988 on page 31 whereas, in a very rough estimate, the railway network occupies probably one hundredth of that area. Second, the air transport operators have the unique bonus of that third dimension, so when we consider volume rather than area the amount of it taken for the task calls for not only an explanation, but some drastic rationalisation. The separation between aircraft under air traffic control that the CAA seek to maintain is normally 5 miles horizontally and 1000 feet vertically, so each aircraft is surrounded by some 30 cubic miles of otherwise empty airspace; since there are more than 75,000 cubic miles of airways above Great Britain, at least 2500 airliners can be accommodated within them before they can be called 'saturated'. In short, although in fatality rate terms the figures for both modes are broadly similar, the low level of accuracy with which air navigation and aircraft operation can be achieved in such safety reveals a grossly excessive use of a finite commodity – the usable parts of the sky above our heads. This is an important point for anyone who is seriously interested in the overall safety levels of *all* aviation activities, including general aviation and the air transport sector, so later I return to the subject in an attempt to put the requirements into balance.

There is one other way, however, in which air travel could be made even safer than it is, but here commercial competition plays the leading role. All passenger transport aircraft operated by the Royal Air Force have rearward facing seats, for clearly in the case of very rapid deceleration the protection that these offer can save lives and avoid or reduce injuries, but the Service is not worried by the need to sell tickets to people who have choices of carrier. Most probably, if one civil operator adopted this principle and plugged the idea as a safety feature, it would prove to be a success in business terms so others would follow; but then the required sales publicity would awaken the dormant fear that lurks in some people and the whole subject of safety – which leads the mind to the possible lack of it – might be brought into play unnecessarily. An inescapable fact, though, is that passengers travelling 'with their backs to the engine' are more likely to avoid harm than those facing forward. Probably the safest seats on public sale (which, alas, the RAF ones are not) are those facing rearward and adjoining the central open corridor on British trains, on which the passenger survival rate following impact is almost unbelievably high. One advantage that air travel can claim over rail, however, is that all passengers must have seats, whereas the recent increase in demand for rail travel – which, incidentally, quietly surpasses the much publicised rise in demand for movement by air – means that some travellers in trains are required to stand. In fact, in supply/demand assessments, as a practical economic necessity, British Rail take on an expected number of unseated passengers for calculated (but in fact often longer) distances on commuter services, but clearly this must reduce safety standards.

I am sorry that this chapter has contained so much about accidents and deaths, but the point of it all is to bring home one significant fact: that although there are lots of both around us in our daily lives, hardly any of either occurs in any form of air transport. Long may air and rail travel compete to hold the top two places in the transport safety league.

Chapter 4
Avoidable Problems

NOT VERY LONG AGO any pilot, whether commercial, military or private, could fly his aeroplane in a straight line along his intended track from the point of departure to his destination. This caused a broad spread of aerial activity over most parts of the British Isles. Unlike cars and boats, aircraft have the great advantage of that third dimension, so if as an example we take a height band of, say, 20,000 feet and give the approved and generous allowance of 1,000 feet of vertical separation, we have almost 20 times as much space in which to place our air traffic than we have in terms of available surface area. As I mentioned in Chapter 1, we have a recognised and simple system of quadrantal heights at which to fly, so a very substantial number of aircraft can be accommodated with very little likelihood of conflict. As it is, there are relatively few aircraft about so there should be an enormous amount of airspace in which to accommodate them.

Unfortunately that freedom to fly from point to point has been eroded at an alarmingly rapid rate as has the volume of airspace in which aircraft are *allowed* to fly. As evidence to support this, I ask you to look at the accompanying diagrams showing the amounts of controlled airspace over the UK in 1950, 1960, 1970, 1980 and 1988. In case you feel that these malignant growths have been exaggerated to help to press a point, let me add that they are reproduced as published by the CAA (CAP 540: Air Traffic Management in the UK) and they have received no medical attention. In practice, the position for the average general aviation pilot is even worse than the plans depict, for they do not mark danger areas, military training areas or other places around which careful avoidance planning is required.

The continued expansion in the amount of regulated airspace over the UK is causing more and more people to ask whether it has achieved its objective of increasing safety for all users. Whilst all changes are made for the apparent benefit of the commercial air transport sector, what does this do for the others, whom we must not forget constitute the majority? These aircraft are compressed involuntarily into corridors, corners and tunnels and, whereas in former years their pilots would have been able to go about their flying with relative ease and in almost total safety, today they need to devote time and attention to constant changes of heading and height. In practice, especially in the London area, the pattern is very complex and the topographical chart used for visual navigation has become so cluttered that it is virtually unreadable. See page 32.

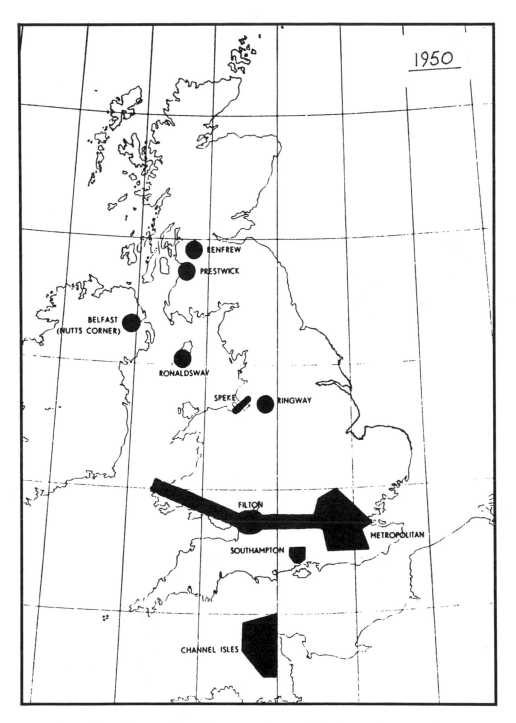

These five charts show just how the cancer of controlled airspace has grown in 40 years, mostly to protect the 700 or so commercial transport aircraft from the legitimate operations of over 11,000 General Aviation aircraft. (Courtesy Civil Aviation Authority)

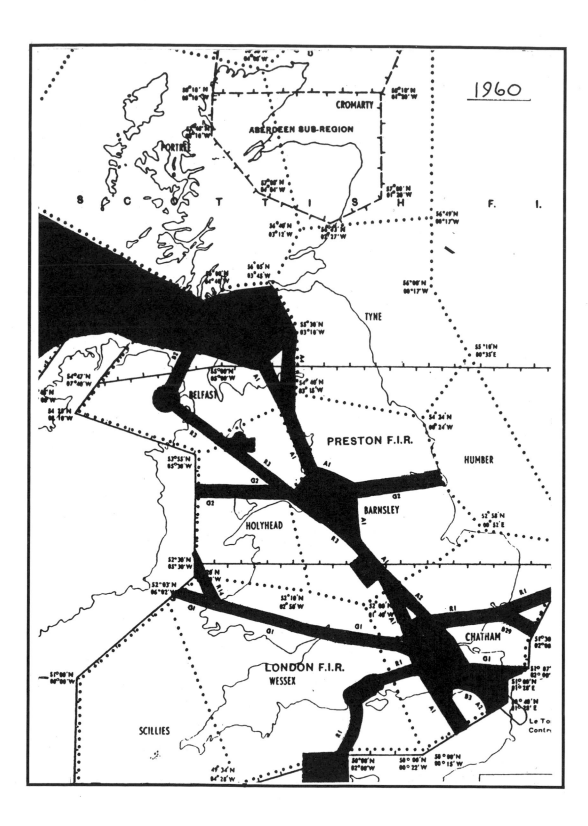

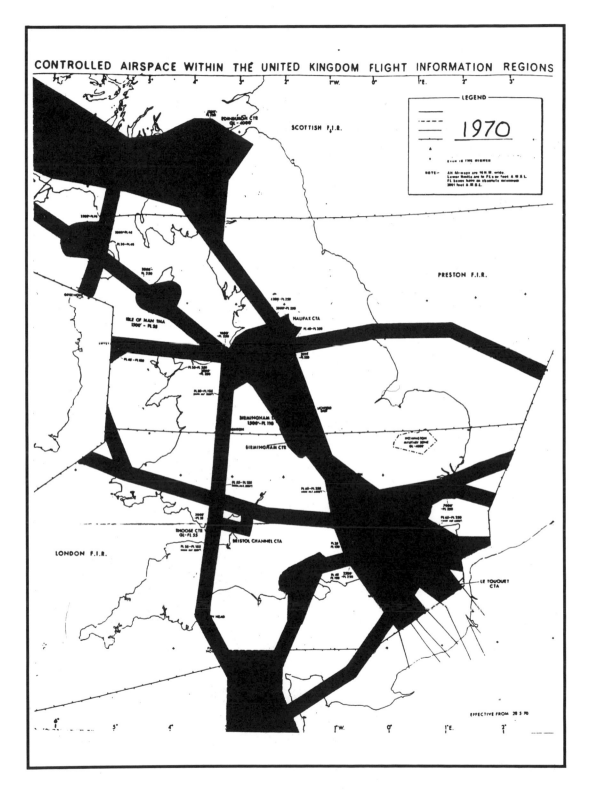

CONTROLLED AIRSPACE WITHIN THE UNITED KINGDOM FLIGHT INFORMATION REGIONS

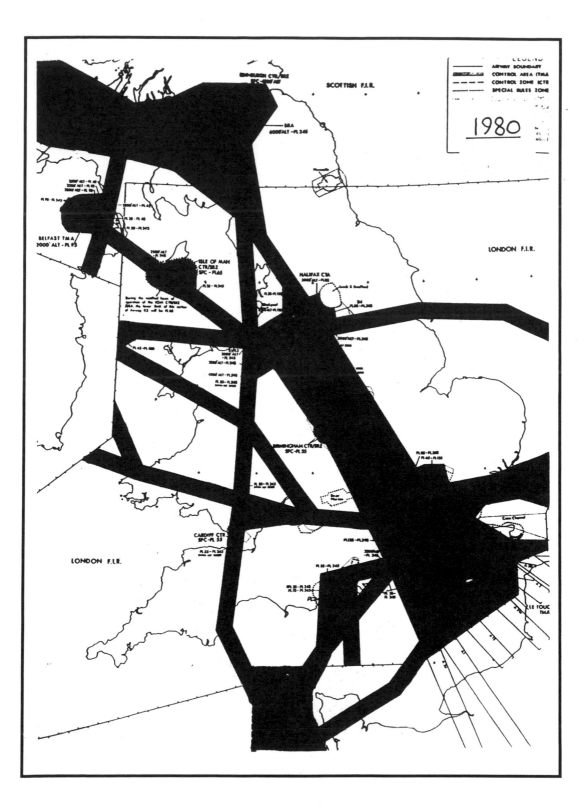

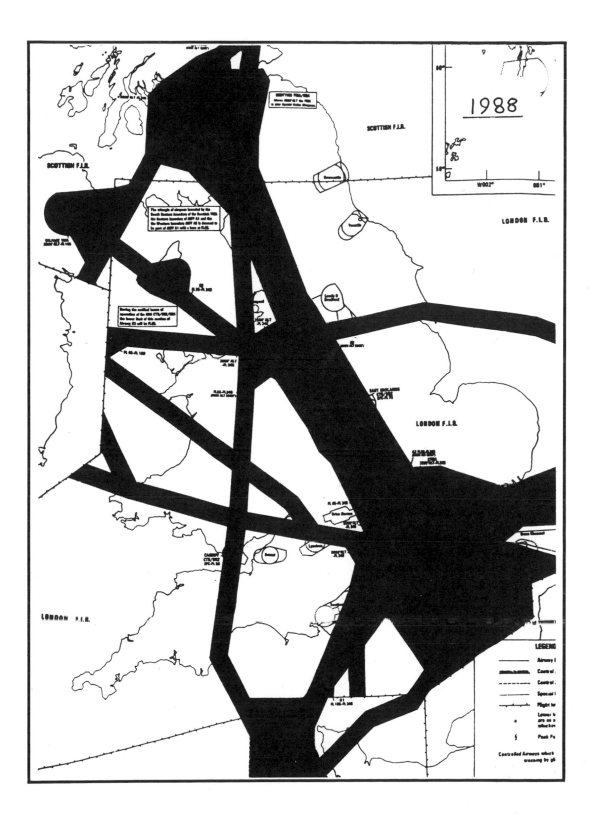

This composite map, showing recent changes in the London Terminal Manoeuvring Area, shows clearly the confusion that confronts pilots who endeavour to navigate by map reading over this corner of South-East England. (Courtesy NATS)

As a result of all this, the GA pilot who does all the right things in the right places is so occupied that he has very little spare capacity with which to concentrate on looking outside for other aircraft. Conversely if he keeps his eyes open to avoid possible conflict, he is liable to stray into a forbidden area and face the consequences. Very few pilots penetrate controlled airspace by intent and although a captain must be responsible for the safe passage of his ship, the number of reported incidents shows that the system is virtually unworkable. Whilst one cannot condone an offender's actions, almost always these are not of his own choosing and if NATS and the CAA have a serious desire to improve safety, as a matter of some urgency they have a responsibility to reduce the present complexity.

In the past, several suggestions have been made, but to put these into practice would be uncomfortable to many who see airspace and air traffic control as entities in themselves. Unfortunately, although air traffic control exists with the statutory duty ' . . . to expedite the flow of air traffic' (incidentally, all traffic, not just selected traffic) and therefore should be seen in its correct context as a facility that exists to serve the user, there are increasing numbers who lose sight of this purpose. As one member of NATS staff explained to me, not so long ago many of his colleagues were operations officers, most of whom were former (and some still current) fliers, while progressively their places in the planning corridors have been taken by controllers. Here again the problem increases, for as one very senior and broad-minded controller pointed out, when he joined the air traffic system he and nearly all his associates were former aircrew, who, to use his own words, 'had been about a bit'. Now, through no fault on their parts, he said, most of the present band of controllers have no experience in other spheres and see their work in a much narrower light. They are known to spend much of their spare time in mutual social activity which tends to contract the mental vision still further. The speaker was generalising, of course, and there are some excellent people who see their duties as being to help those in the air, but from letters and other information that I have received they recognise that they are in the minority. One wrote to say that many of his associates tend to control traffic that it is not their job to control, with the result that pilots feel that much of the responsibility for the safety of a flight is taken away, creating a false feeling of security. This can have repetitive and confusing effects concerning who is responsible for what. Not surprisingly, the author of this letter asked that his name should be withheld 'for fear of castigation by the people with whom I work'.

With the basic problem of seeing airspace management and control as its own entity and with many controllers getting no closer to aviation than seeing aircraft as blips on radar screens, we must not be too surprised when we find that planning is carried out on a piecemeal basis, with computer simulations of projected traffic levels playing leading roles in the thinking process. Of course such exercises have important parts to play, but often the reality of the world outside is overlooked and certainly there are tendencies in many quarters to forget that the demands of airspace come from many more users than from the relatively small number of airliners. When a study was carried out recently on the Cross Channel Special Rules Area – invented originally to protect commercial air traffic that ceased to operate several years ago – a shock came when the results proved that of 20,000 annual aircraft movements, only one per cent (200 in a year or little more than one flight on each alternate day) came in the commercial air transport category! Now a part of this area has been released from restriction, but 33 the general aviation movement needed to press for several years before the study was carried out, the truth revealed and appropriate action taken.

Not only GA suffers from inadequacies in airspace layout. An example of lack of liaison with users concerns Standard Instrument Departures (SIDs). These are procedures used by commercial air transport pilots when climbing after take-off and heading towards the airways system, but in certain conditions of weight and temperature at least two types in current airline service are unable to conform. As one aggrieved controller said to me 'these SIDs are controller-designed within NATS. Who there has any expertise on aircraft performance?' Most modern aircraft, however, do have climb rates far in excess of the requirements to enable them to conform, and another angle is reflected in these comments from Dick Barnby, based on his many years' experience as a controller at Gatwick:

> With the introduction of the SIDS it would have been an ideal opportunity to have updated the vertical profile of the standard routes. The heights at which aircraft were required to cross specific reporting points were, and still are, based upon the performance of aircraft that were already obsolete. Thirty years ago the average rate of climb of a commercial aircraft was not greatly in excess of 500 to 600 ft a minute; now many aircraft fully loaded can well exceed 4000 ft a minute and even the Dash 7 can better 1500 ft per minute, yet the SIDs are calculated on a rate of climb of 500 ft.
>
> Were the vertical profiles of the SIDs to be adjusted to reflect the actual performance of modern aircraft, then the base of the TMA could well be raised by as much as 1000 to 1500 ft at no disadvantage to aircraft within the TMA. It can be argued that there are some aircraft which, while wishing to use the TMA, could not meet the revised heights; even under the existing SIDs there are some aeroplanes that claim not to be able to comply with the SIDs, but in general it is the manner in which the aircraft are operated which governs their performance. The B747 is often quoted as being unable to comply with existing SIDs and some of the early 747s under certain weather conditions might have had problems; however this is no reason for failing to modify the SIDs so as to reflect the performance of modern aircraft. It is nothing new for an aircraft which cannot meet the existing requirements to accept delays and/or extended routing.

In general, changes to regulated airspace are made by adding little (and sometimes not-so-little) pieces here and there onto the existing pattern. This is a relatively easy task and therefore is undertaken in preference to examining the whole system and planning accordingly. Several years ago a statistician declared that if all existing controlled airspace was withdrawn and each aircraft flew directly from its point of departure to its destination on a quadrantal height, the likelihood of collision would be considerably less than it is with the present complex system of control, which creates artificial congestion at beacons and reporting points. Predictably, despite publicity for the idea, no action was taken, but in 1988 further suggestions were made, including a proposal to delete all but a small area of controlled airspace around each *major* airport; this would include the extension of the runway centreline to protect aircraft on their instrument approaches, which would become the only sections of airspace to continue to carry considerable traffic levels. Some months later I heard that one person in NATS (an Operations Officer) had started with a clean chart and was working on

just such a scheme until he was told by his superior (a controller) to stop wasting time. It is not difficult to see why such a straightforward scheme would be highly unpopular with those whose primary task in life is to plan the pattern.

Unfortunately the complexity of the present airspace system, especially in the south-east, creates a range of other problems that are imposed on the majority: the general aviation pilots. When political or commercial pressures are more powerful than those applied by the people actively involved, many strange and unacceptable proposals follow. At any time several ideas are wafting about in the planning pipe and sometimes there are difficulties in assessing which to take seriously and which can be relegated safely to the mental slow-burner. Almost two years ago there were preliminary references to the 'need' for adjustments to the London Terminal Manoeuvring Area (LTMA) and several possible proposals were shunted about. Nothing was offered as a definitive plan and, possibly by intent, confusion arose among those out in the real world who must assess the seriousness of the impact of any projected scheme. One set of proposals that had 'appeared' but not been circulated to most people concerned, was being discussed in some quarters and some very valid reasons for objection were being prepared when, in December 1988, a plan showing different changes went on the more formal official rounds. Despite the differences, NATS attempted to evade the customary consultation period on the grounds that everyone had received adequate warning of proposed change, and only after pressure from within the GA movement was a nominal allowance of two months given for everyone to come back with objections. I say 'nominal' because the shock announcement was issued shortly before Christmas (a practice that has occurred before and has not passed unnoticed) when organised liaison between the affected bodies and their memberships would be difficult to arrange. Prior to this the delay had been excused on the grounds that the CAA element within NATS had asked the Department of Transport to approve the proposal and was awaiting a response. That argument was considered to be suspect, however, and when Ron Campbell, in his capacity as European Regional Co-ordinator for the International Council of Aircraft Owner and Pilot Associations, wrote to the Department for clarification, these words came in the reply from the Civil Aviation Policy Division: 'Decisions on airspace are for the Civil Aviation Authority and the National Air Traffic Services. In accordance with Ministerial directions made in 1976, the planning of airspace arrangements must take account of the requirements of all users, including general aviation'.

Further investigation began to unearth the unhealthy inner workings. The proposal placed before the flying fraternity would lower the base of the LTMA in two large and critical areas of Kent, amounting to a reduction of 3.25 billion cubic feet in the airspace available for use by most GA aircraft. This is one of the few heavily used areas, where flying training, business and other essential non-airline traffic has substantial airspace requirements and this is growing at a more rapid rate than is the case with the much-publicised commercial air transport sector. In short, despite a need for more space as demand increases, these aircraft would be squeezed into tighter corners. For example, if the base of the TMA is at 3,500 feet, operations can be carried out over a maximum height spread of about 2,000 feet, using 1,500 feet above ground level or above the highest object en route as the absolute practical minimum. So a reduction in ceiling from 3,500 to 2,500 feet (which was the case here) removes 50 per cent of the usable space and this prevents certain essential training exercises from being carried out. The choice remaining is to fly to an area a long way from the home base, which substantially increases the cost of pilot training and possibly 35

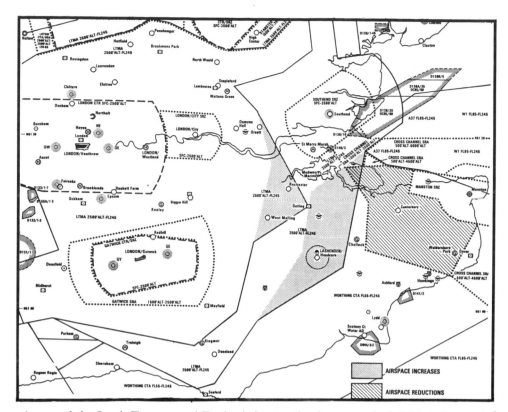

A map of the South-East area of England showing the changes to the LTMA discussed in the adjacent text. This map, incidentally, shows the same 'airspace' information as the previous one, but without the benefit of topographical detail. (Courtesy NATS)

overcrowds an area already in use by other operators; to carry out the exercises at heights lower than sound airmanship and commonsense dictate; or to climb into forbidden territory. The last of these, though illegal, holds an attraction for many because stories abound about large lumps of regulated airspace that are not used by anyone. Continually we are told that airspace is finite and therefore it is in short supply, but only GA users seem to be aware of the amount that is wasted.

Another example of the lowered safety standards that result from such a proposition concerns the pilot in a single-engine aeroplane who plans to cross London on a north-south axis. If he is refused permission to do so at a height that enables him to abide by the requirement to glide to open country in the event of engine failure, his only practical alternative is to find an outlet to the east and fly over 30 miles of water (longer than a Channel crossing) to travel between two neighbouring English aerodromes. On safety grounds alone, quite apart from cost and inconvenience, many of us would be very reluctant to do this, possibly to the point of refusal.

This is merely one of a series of organisational mishaps with which those of us who represent the majority of users are compelled to contend; but the story is far from finished. The Rules of the Air state the minimum heights at which pilots may fly over congested areas. A key part of this (Rule 5 (1) (a)) requires anyone flying a single-engine aircraft always to be in a position to glide to open country in the event of a power failure. Public parks, sports grounds and other such welcome sights to the pilot with a problem are excluded from the permitted choice of landing areas, so over a large conurbation a considerable height may be required in order to clear the built-up area; and even when a town is sufficiently small to enable this aspect to be covered from a relatively low level (the minimum permitted is 1,500 feet), an unacceptable restriction on the maximum height at which to fly causes an undesirable noise nuisance to those beneath. So when an aeroplane flies over your home low enough to be noticed, please remember that it may be where it is, not because the pilot wishes to be there, but because the regulations prevent him from flying at a more sensible height.

These two height requirements may be incompatible, but we are forced to operate in a situation in which the left and right hands of authority have little mutual contact. When a controller gives a pilot a clearance to fly on a certain route or through a specific area he is doing so purely on the basis of separation from other known traffic. He may give that clearance at a height which contravenes the requirements of part of Rule 5 (1) (a) and then the pilot must decide whether he accepts it. Because this may be the only way in which he can cover his required route, frequently he nods a wink at the rule and goes. Although for many years attempts have been made to persuade controllers to give combined airspace/legal height clearances, they have refused resolutely to do so. There have been cases in which pilots have been given air traffic clearances and then, despite following them precisely, have been prosecuted for failing to abide by the requirements of Rule 5. The route clearance is no defence and the prosecutions have succeeded.

It is strange that one section of the CAA forces unfortunate pilots to fly lower than they would choose, while another section decides to step-up its line of action against those who do as they have been told. This has happened because one pilot – in the only recorded incident of its kind – suspected a cockpit fire, shut down the engine and made an emergency landing on a sports field at Walthamstow. One occupant of the aeroplane was killed, but no-one on the ground suffered injury and a brick wall was the only earthbound casualty. The CAA's alarmist reaction, however, comes as no surprise to those of us who live with such anomalies. When I add that I have met cases in which representatives of one department within the same CAA group have conveniently forgotten to send delegates to another department's meeting, very few surprises remain ahead. Certainly in the case of the 1988/89 plan for cankerous growth to the LTMA, the appropriate people within the Safety Regulation Group of the Authority were not invited to take part and were not even consulted in the original planning stages. They were invited to comment on the finalised plans only shortly before these were circulated to the operating industry. Some who feel well disposed to the trappings of the system may consider this to be a case of British democracy at its very best, but I have heard opinions expressed in markedly different tones. Interestingly, even during the official consultation period, the chart makers agreed that they were busily preparing new maps showing those changes (only proposals, of course) as though they were set hard.

You may be wondering why this particular piece of vandalism to the LTMA was mooted. Most probably you assume that this is to accommodate some of the commercial air traffic operating to and from Heathrow and Gatwick that suffered so much congestion and delay during the summer of 1988. But no! It is primarily for the handful of machines operating out of London City Airport and, secondly, for a few aircraft from Biggin Hill that seek the protection of controlled airspace. So let us take a brief look at each case and the alleged requirement.

The airspace system over Britain has evolved over nearly 40 years and, whatever our personal opinions may be about the way in which it has developed, its purpose is clear and has been based on the known and predicted needs of certain established or long-planned airports. Initially London's regulated area existed for Heathrow and, later, Gatwick joined in. Then Luton began to expand in the commercial air transport business. So a system was assembled to accommodate a mix of traffic from these three airports. Then, when someone decided that London needed a third airport (third in national terms; Luton is of local authority origin) Stansted was fed into the plan. Many people objected to the amount of additional area that was taken for this, but at least it was known to all long before it was introduced and some form of forward planning was possible. Then, right in the middle of it all, as if from nowhere, someone wanted to dig-up a piece of waste ground in the old London dockland and before long a small single airstrip had appeared; this was christened with the rather overscaled title, London City Airport (LCY). No-one with a progressive outlook should scorn the person who sees commercial potential from scrap, but there are ways – and times – in which to do it. No-one planned – and, in fairness to those concerned, no-one had knowledge of the need to plan – to fit this into the London air traffic complex and clearly some eleventh-hour problems arose. In practice, there would have been no difficulty in feeding the paltry amount of traffic into and out of the existing system, but for purposes of political gain (about which I will add more later) – the controllers' union in the form of the Institute of Professional Civil Servants played hard to get and refused to do so. Also, a promised radar guidance and separation service from Gatwick failed to materialise as a part of the plan by the controllers to draw more attention to themselves. But by this time the commercial operators were ready to ply the line between London City and Paris, so they operated underneath the controlled airspace and could have continued to do so without interruption to this day and forever. Foolishly, however, they soiled their own patch by reporting three alleged air-misses as part of their plan to have a piece of the sky to themselves. The short time-scale over which this unpredicted development had taken place was such that the CAA needed to issue free gummed stickers for pilots to place on their (frequently changed) maps, indicating the existence of LCY and the special rules zone (yet *another* piece of controlled airspace) that surrounds it.

Although two of these politically-motivated airmisses were found to be fallacious and the third involved no danger of collision, the damage that they had inflicted on their own cause was sufficient for the Chairman of the CAA to write to the Chairman of Brymon Airways, suspending that company's approval to operate the scheduled service between London City Airport and Paris. A copy of the letter, which was released with a covering news release from the CAA, is reproduced opposite.

After a suitable pause, the flights were reinstated, still in unregulated airspace. At the same time (incidentally substantiating my point about poor lookout) an inadequately worded Aeronautical Information Circular (AIC) was issued on 4th August 1988 containing the advice 'Pilots are reminded that a good lookout should be maintained at all times, when flying in the Flight Information Region, in the vicinity of these routes'. Perhaps I am out-of-date, but I and others of my age were trained to maintain energetic lookouts at all times, regardless of the proximity of other people's routes. Then, towards the end of 1988, the CAA took

CAA▶

Civil Aviation Authority
CAA House
45-59 Kingsway
London WC2B 6TE

Telephone: 01-379 7311

Christopher Tugendhat
Chairman

C Stuart Esq
Chairman
Brymon Aviation Ltd
City Airport
Crownhill
Plymouth
Devon PL6 8BW   18 December 1987

Dear

As you know, at the 1983 Planning Inquiry, the Civil Aviation
Authority made it clear that National Air Traffic Services
would be unable to contain London City Airport traffic within
the London Terminal Manoeuvring Area until the 1990's, when the
planned Central Control Function will start to take effect. It
is by no means unusual for traffic using an airport not to have
access to controlled airspace. Although traffic in the South
East of England is very heavy, aircraft using LCY fly in an
environment which is not essentially different from that in
which international scheduled operations are conducted to and
from other airports in the United Kingdom and abroad. Having
flown on flights operated to and from LCY by both Eurocity
Express and Brymon Airways, the Authority's Flight Operations
Inspectorate are of the view that there is nothing unusual in
the circumstances in which LCY services are operated.

However, since LCY operations began in October you have written
12 letters, either to me or to my officials expressing concern
about the safety of LCY operations. Moreover, on 30 October
1987 Captain H Gee, your Flight Operations Manager stated in a
minute to you "From the time Thames Radar Services terminated
to the time London Control actually do start controlling there
are no radar advisories and we are on our own "eyeballing" our
way along in unprotected airspace which is an area of intense
training and on occasions gliding activity. In my professional
opinion this is a most unsatisfactory and dangerous manner
in which to conduct a Public Transport Operation and I feel it
is incumbent upon the Authority to provide a measure of
protection that ensures the safety of ours and Eurocity's
operation. We require at least TMA base plus 500ft until
clearance to join airways is given". At a meeting with Mr
Toseland, the Authority's Joint Field Commander, on 15
December, Captain Gee said that unless there was a positive
improvement in air traffic services within 28 days he would be
forced to recommend your Board to suspend LCY services. The

(Cont. over)

39

Eurocity Express representatives at the meeting did not dissent from this view expressed by Captain Gee. At our meeting today you made it clear that your and Captain Gee's concern was with the safety of operations on the LCY/Paris route and that if NATS had provided the same level of air traffic service on that route as is provided on the LCY/Brussels route your letters would not have neen written. A further consideration is that three airmisses have been reported by pilots of aircraft en route to or from LCY, 2 of them in the week beginning 7 December.

While NATS will as before continue to use its best endeavours it cannot for the time being guarantee a permanent and systematic upgrading of air traffic services.

The Authority cannot ignore your concern as Chairman of Brymon Airways, the twice repeated professional advice of someone with Captain Gee's experience, in particular his practical experience over the last two months of LCY operations, or the three reported airmisses. In the light of those matters the Authority cannot at present be satisfied that any operator is competent to secure the safe operation of aircraft on public transport flights between LCY and Paris.

Accordingly, the Authority, in exercise of its powers under Article 62 of the Air Navigation Order 1985 and Regulation 6(8)(a) of the Civil Aviation Authority Regulations 1983 hereby provisionally varies the air operator's certificate held by Brymon Aviation Limited by adding the following condition:-

> "No flight for the purpose of public transport
> may be made between London City Airport and Paris".

pending inquiry into and consideration of the case.

The inquiry will focus on the facts surrounding the airmisses and the basis for Captain Gee's opinion. If that opinion proves to be well founded the Authority will have to consider attaching the aforesaid condition to your company's Air Operator's Certificate until such time as LCY traffic can be contained within the LTMA.

Yours sincerely

CHRISTOPHER TUGENDHAT

the previously unknown step of marking the likely tracks of these aircraft on the half-million-scale topographical chart of southern England. By this time the commercial pressure was having its effect on the politicians, who in turn shifted some of the load onto the airspace planners; so in December 1988 a document issued by NATS declared that the strictly commercial venture of an airport at docklands had become Government policy! Therefore, suddenly, action became necessary. Irreverent stories abound following such shenanigans: one is that the main reason for the operator's insistence on being allowed into controlled airspace is that the increased height would enable stewardesses to pour drinks without the problems of the bumps encountered at lower levels.

One measure adopted by Mowlem, the owners and operators of London City, in seeking support for their plans, was to send a circular letter to all the property developers in Docklands. Fortunately, however, I received a copy via one recipient who was well out of sympathy with the Mowlem aims. In it the company urges commercial developers to support not only the expansion of the LTMA but also 'the planned growth of London City Airport'. This is especially interesting in view of the predicted reductions in demand for air travel between London and the near Continental destinations when the channel tunnel takes its share of the load. This, incidentally, is a subject that is virtually verboten in discussions with the airspace planners, who tend to draw imaginative projections showing endless expansion. This is precisely the mistake made by the designers of our northern motorways, which have proved to be expensively overdesigned for capacities that cannot possibly be needed. Can we not learn from the disastrous errors of others?

The Biggin Hill side of the story is much shorter. Here the management had pressed NATS into providing a means by which operators of business aircraft (there are no scheduled services) would be able to climb through and descend via regulated airspace into and out of the airways system. In isolation, this sounds fine, but it imposes a heavy penalty on the scope of operation for by far the majority of the aircraft owners and operators based at Biggin. Certainly the flying training organisations are wholly out of sympathy with this change and they (who generate by far the greater amount of the traffic and revenue) will be among the many sufferers caught in the trap of needing to fly further from home in order to carry out certain exercises in the pilot training syllabus. This they will be forced to do in the more congested surroundings of the reduced area that will be available to them.

This chapter has centred mainly on just one problem that the wishes of a few have imposed on a growing majority, but it shows an example of ill-conceived planning that may marginally increase convenience for a chosen handful, but which clearly will drastically reduce safety for most. The final plan was rushed into action on a panic basis from initial detailed announcement in December 1988 to a scheduled introduction in April 1989. Fortunately most of the nation's many GA organisations combined their individual strengths into a force of power and confronted NATS with their fears about the danger of collision that the scheme would create. Despite these warnings from those who represent the majority of airspace users and who know what is needed, the proposals were implemented.

The two examples above have caused considerable concern among the growing GA fraternity and I quote here just two examples of the many feelings that have been expressed. Firstly, a letter that I received from Dick Barnby, whose opinion is of especial value, as he has been an air traffic controller and watch supervisor at Gatwick Airport:

The recent steps taken by the Civil Aviation Authority, to accommodate the trickle of traffic using the London City Airport, highlight only too well the attitude of the Authority towards General Aviation, and what is more the safety of General Aviation.

The introduction of yet more controlled airspace in the already congested South Eastern corner of the UK is a totally unwarranted burden for General Aviation.

If it had been impossible for the City Airport traffic to be accommodated within existing controlled airspace, then possibly General Aviation users might well have been prepared to accept yet more restrictions, in the way of yet more controlled airspace. As it is there is no reason why this traffic could not have been, quite safely, accommodated within existing controlled airspace.

It has been said that the traffic generated by the London City airport represented the straw that would have broken the back of the LATCC camel. This is rubbish, for if the LATCC controllers are so hard pushed that they are unable to cope with the traffic from City airport, does this mean that LATCC will be unable to handle any more traffic out of Gatwick or Heathrow?

If it does, then regardless of what we have been led to believe, the delays for the happy holiday makers will be even worse than they were in this past summer.

A lot could well be done to improve the situation, were ATCOs, in general, to have a fundamental change in attitude towards General Aviation. From day one they should be taught to recognise the fact that General Aviation has as much right to the sky as has Commercial Aviation. The whole question of controlled airspace needs to be examined in the light of the performance of modern-day jet aircraft. Once and for all the ghost of the York 'on three' or the Dakota 'on one' should be laid to rest. Then and only then can we hope to see any improvement in the lot of the General Aviation operator.

[These last comments refer to earlier aircraft types with marginal performance when one engine had failed, eg a four-engined York with only three engines operating. D.O.]

Now to John Ward, the Chairman of the General Aviation Safety Committee, who expressed these views in the Spring 1989 issue of the Flight Safety Bulletin:

In the Winter 1988/89 issue of the *Flight Safety Bulletin* on page 32 we published the details of the three routes and heights that Dash 7 aircraft operating out of London (City) Airport would follow during the brief period that they had to fly in the FIR while on their way to and from the Continent. The hope was that general aviation aircraft flying in the area would either avoid these routes or, when this was not possible, keep an especially sharp look out for Dash 7s which, after all, are not the World's fastest aircraft. We were under the impression that this had been accepted by the Dash 7 operators as a reasonably satisfactory solution to the problem, which seemed to be confirmed by the reduction in the number of airmisses filed by Dash 7 pilots following the original spate.

How wrong we were! In a letter dated 9th December 1988, the Chairman of the National Air Traffic Management Advisory Committee (NATMAC) sent to members of that Committee proposals to lower the base of the London TMA by 1,000 feet over a large area of Kent so as to allow the Dash 7s to operate continuously within the cosiness of controlled airspace. For good measure, a need to accommodate IFR traffic operating into and out of Biggin Hill was thrown in. As a sop to general aviation, it also was proposed to deregulate a part of the Cross Channel Special Rules Airspace over east Kent.

Despite the objections of a number of general aviation organisations that these proposals would increase safety for a few for a disproportionate loss of safety for many, and various alternative suggestions to reduce the impact on general aviation, the powers that be in the National Air Traffic Services (NATS) have now decided that, as from 6th April 1989, their original proposals will come into effect. So if you are obliged to operate below the TMA in this area after that date, you are advised to keep a particularly sharp look out for other traffic and make the maximum use of your radio if you have one.

An aspect of this affair that has caused further concern is the nature and time allowed for what is somewhat euphemistically called 'the consultation process'. In the Summer 1987 issue of this Bulletin on page 33 we drew attention to the inadequacy of the present procedure. This was in connection with another occasion when there was a large increase in the size of the London TMA and associated airspace, described then as 'changes', which came into effect on 7th May 1987 with little time for general aviation to assess the consequences and no time for adequate warning. As a result of an approach to the NATMAC Chairman, it was agreed that notification of proposed changes to Regulated Airspace which affected UK general aviation would be given in the CAA's General Aviation Safety Information leaflets with an indication of where details of the proposals could be seen. Unfortunately, following a token announcement to this effect, nothing further has happened. So we propose to try again because, although the present procedure may be adequate for small close-knit organisations like airlines, it is totally inadequate for a widespread and diverse organisation such as the general aviation movement.

So, on safety grounds, GA was and is far from happy. However, following further pressure from users, NATS have agreed to form a working party that will enable the two sides to look again at the overall picture. Perhaps then they will consider implementing their own policy, published in the NATS Operational Strategy Plan dated September 1988:

'NATS airspace planning to the year 2000 is based upon the premise that as far as possible airspace will be developed to meet the fundamental requirements of the three major groups of users: public transport, military and general aviation . . . . In the past, compromise has been manifested in a segregation of airspace to separate the different users; *for the future the greater emphasis will be placed on the sharing of airspace to the mutual benefit of all users.*' [italics are mine : D.O.]

The final changes to the LTMA were announced only three months later than that policy statement and were in direct conflict with its message, but now, airspace users await the results of that new dawn . . . .

Chapter 5
The Villain
of the Piece?

UNDERSTANDABLY many people, including some who earn their livings in aviation, believe that all unacceptable plans and proposals for restrictions emanate from the CAA. After reading the previous chapter, readers may shudder with surprise when I move to the defence of the Authority, but I must make clear that ideas originate from a wide range of sources. Many come from those with vested interests in protecting their own positions or even their pensions. Unfortunately, whatever the source and however impracticable the proposal, time and effort are required by the operators' negotiators (many of whom tackle these tasks voluntarily and in their spare time) in attempts to prevent the damage that the idea might inflict upon the people most concerned – the airspace users.

One problem in the planning process concerns the dog, its tail and who does the wagging. Not many years ago most moves were made in the interests of the people for whom the airspace exists: those who fly in it. Already I have mentioned the progressive changes within NATS that have reduced its level of pilot representation to becoming an organisation with essentially controller-based thinking; this has led to proposals for change emanating, not from those who need to operate in the affected areas, but from others whose primary task should be to provide a service for those users. Unfortunately, though, this degradation is not restricted to official levels, for it has extended to private organisations that have their own reasons for wishing to impose their wishes on others.

A case that comes to mind immediately is one that received some sour comment in the aviation press. Members of The Guild of Air Traffic Control Officers (GATCO) took it upon themselves to suggest that the airspace used by up to 35 aerodromes with published instrument approach procedures should become regulated. This would impose long narrow arms of virtually no-go areas for most users, adding to the complexity of the task of flying from one point to another over a country that already has a plethora of restrictions that lead to confusion. No pilots had asked for this. It was put forward for the convenience of controllers whose duties would be lightened if the bulk of the nation's aircraft – GA and Military – could be squeezed out of their particular patches. Not surprisingly the idea received a fairly hostile reception from the people who would be affected, with the Aircraft Owners and Pilots Association (AOPA) and the Guild of Air Pilots and Air Navigators (GAPAN) reacting with alternative propositions. Both organisations offered reasoned arguments against the idea of even more regulated airspace and eventually a working group was formed in an attempt to reach some form of compromise solution. Apart from AOPA and GAPAN, clearly the Ministry of Defence wished to see no extension of the existing restrictions on their activities, but apparently they offered remarkably little in the way of front-line fighting. When I repeat the relative figures that I mentioned in an earlier chapter, the reason for the strength of the opposition to the idea becomes clear: with perhaps 1500 military aircraft and 10,000 GA machines, nearly all of which *need* to operate in free airspace, we have about 11,500 aircraft whose pilots would be seriously handicapped by the plan if implemented and fewer than 700 machines that could use the numerous chunks of sheltered accommodation, but as more than half of these operate on main-line services between major airports such as Heathrow, Gatwick, Manchester, Birmingham and others that have more than adequate protection already, probably fewer than 200 aircraft in total would make use of such a facility; and *none* of their pilots has asked for it.

Over a period of many months discussions continued. The Aerodrome Owners Association (AOA) chose to take sides with GATCO, partially because the former had many members of the latter on their staffs and then the British Airline Pilots Association (BALPA) came into the foray on behalf of the minority of their members who might be involved. Clearly the two sides were firmly entrenched and the responsibility fell squarely upon the shoulders of NATS to find a solution; and here I wish to be very fair to that body, for the officers concerned tackled the task in a wholly open and unbiased way. As the proposal had come from an outside agency and not from any official source, they were in a position to see the situation in a clear perspective. They called for more evidence to support the proposition and Exeter Airport, for one, went to considerable lengths to record every incident that had occurred in their vicinity. The result, though, was quite the opposite to the one that they had hoped, for a close analysis of each case revealed that there was no common cause; this helped to strengthen the opposition's argument that (a) there was no need for change and (b) if implemented, it could not provide a solution to any problems if they exist. Interestingly, the final report contained a sentence to the effect that Exeter's findings served to show that by informing pilots about possible traffic conflicts, the airport's controllers were doing merely what they were there to do. Some people have asked whether GATCO'S proposal was intended primarily to relieve the members from undertaking what – after all – is their primary responsibility. No-one seems to know, for no convincing reason was put forward in the first place.

After more than a year a proposal was submitted and accepted as a typical British compromise. Clearly there was no justification for an increase in the amount of regulated airspace, but agreement was reached that instrument approach lanes would be marked on topographical charts for those aerodromes that required this and non-participating pilots would be advised (not compelled) to avoid these where it was practicable to do so. Also, as added guidelines, easily recognisable visual reporting points (VRPs) would be agreed and pilots would route via these to and from the places concerned. Here, though, the cake crumbled still further, for of the 35 aerodromes that had been identified as needing instrument approach protection, when asked to agree to the idea fewer than half showed any interest in introducing VRPs and pressures were applied to others in a last minute attempt to prevent the total collapse of the case. Final ignominy was reached, however, when only four aerodromes wanted to adopt the idea of visual routings (VR) to and from those points! Interestingly, this could be because VRPs and VRs are known by many users to offer disadvantages as well as benefits. They force well-spread traffic to converge on single spots and therefore create unnecessary conflict, with totally unoccupied airspace on all sides. At some places the mandatory reporting points are known as the only pieces of congested airspace in their respective counties!

So what started as a fairly feeble politically-motivated proposal ended as a very wet squib, but it occupied the time and attention of many people who could have devoted their minds and energies to more productive purposes. If the scheme had been accepted it would have increased the workload for substantial numbers of pilots and as every person has a finite level of mental capacity, any enforced activity increase leaves a reduced amount that is available for navigation, lookout and other essentials for safe flight. Unfortunately, however, the scheme's protagonists seem to be unhappy with the democratically-decided conclusion and now they are planning other routes through which to seek to attain their objectives.

Although this tale has been heard in many places and has been told in sections through various parts of the technical press, here I have assembled the whole sad truth, for it goes some way towards revealing the unhealthy atmosphere that prevails in aviation as a grossly dismembered body that seems quite unable to live and work with itself. When I add that, throughout the period of discussion and negotiation, the project was kept closely to the NATS chest and the CAA's specialist aerodromes section was not even asked for an opinion, my point is strengthened further.

Some proposals that emanate from the provinces are requests – amounting sometimes almost to demands – for protected airspace around regional airports. In a later chapter I give some details of the aircraft movements and numbers of passengers carried at various places and, especially when we compare these figures with other transport modes, we cannot escape realising that air travel is an embarassingly small-scale operation. Despite the unimpressive figures, however, commercial air transport is the largest space-consumer and until more efficient and accurate navigational and separation methods are available, even the few movements that occur now at the regionals are causing their operators to seek the creation of restricted airspace that handicaps the other users.

One case that caused much discussion centres on Newcastle, where the airport operator decided that because of the traffic growth in recent years, the dimensions of the regulated airspace around it should be extended. Already the airport enjoyed a special rules area (SRA) with a base of 1500 feet and pilots on north-south (or vice-versa) routes could travel safely just below this height, routing inland of the coast. The proposal, though, was to enlarge the more restrictive special rules zone (SRZ) which extends from the surface to flight level 75 (in round terms, 7500 feet) and this would grow eastwards to a point just *outside* the coastline. Therefore any pilot unable to communicate with or obtain clearance from Newcastle would be forced to fly over the sea, but as still he would be under the SRA he would need to remain below 1500 feet. This, clearly, is not conducive to safety when we contemplate the possibility of engine failure at relatively low level, over the water and possibly in the depths of winter. You may ask why the transit could not be carried out to the west, but on this side there is a combination of high ground, obstructions, a danger area and a gliding site, so in many weather conditions this could be more hazardous than crossing the water.

Unfortunately, despite objections from pilot representative bodies, this change was implemented. Its effect on regular operations has been minimised by local agreements and I have received several favourable comments about the co-operative way in which the controllers handle requests, but in such a situation there will remain the more distant operator whose freedom to travel without undue concern for procedural practices will have been eroded. I quote this as an example of localised requests for regulated airspace that arise in many parts of the UK and not as an isolated criticism of Newcastle. When we look more deeply at the number of movements that take place at most regional airports we will be able to assess more readily whether requests for added protection warrant serious consideration.

My main point in this chapter is to make clear that proposals for change are not necessarily born in the inner sancta of NATS, the CAA or any other statutory body. They may come from unions (about which more is to be revealed), controllers or regional airports; but only very rarely do they originate among pilots, the users, for whom the airspace and its various trappings exist. When I mention pilots, I mean those in all spheres of aviation activity and, to indicate that I have endeavoured to collate opinions from all quarters, I end this section by quoting a senior British Airways captain, whom I met by chance in purely social surroundings. I probed a little and discovered that he was not one of the many airline pilots who indulge in private flying as a relief from the monotony of the task, so I expected him to be a stout defender of the proposed extension to the LTMA. I asked his views and I cannot resist quoting his brisk reply: 'There is about twice as much controlled airspace over the UK as is needed. It needs cleaning-up and managing properly'.

Chapter 6
Airmisses –
Why the Drama?

THERE ARE MANY ways in which aircraft and their occupants can come to grief, but an airmiss is not one. No one can be hurt, let alone killed, in an airmiss, so why do we read and hear so much fuss and drama about what, in effect, must be the ultimate in fail-safe systems? If the alleged incident is genuine – and many are not – it may be the result of a failure on someone's part, but by virtue of what it is, it cannot be, nor can it cause, an accident.

The main reason that most people know the word 'airmiss' is because of excessive and artificial drama generated by certain sections of the media. In the next chapter I will put this into context, but before we look at that you may find some help in knowing what an airmiss is, how it is reported and what happens in the subsequent investigation. Although as a member of the General Aviation Safety Committee I have direct dealings with the subject, I am pleased to have obtained permission from Group Captain John Maitland, who is Officer Commanding the Joint Airmiss Section, to reproduce here the text of a lecture that he gave to the Royal Aeronautical Society on 9th May 1988. This places the entire subject in balance and I could not hope to match it for accuracy:

In the current atmosphere of frequent and mainly exaggerated reports about airmisses in most of the media – I exclude the specialist aviation journals from the charge –I hope this lecture will be useful in giving an accurate idea of the why and how of airmiss investigation in the UK. So I will cover the work of the joint airmiss section, which I have looked after for some two and half years and will probably stay with for another three, and will give an idea of how the joint airmiss working group (the JAWG) goes about its business. I will also give you a feel for the statistics and the background of airmisses.

First, then, let's consider why we should investigate airmisses at all; indeed, what is an airmiss? The definition to which we work in both civil and military publications is 'that an airmiss takes place when, in the opinion of a pilot, his aircraft may have been endangered during flight by the proximity of another aircraft so that a definite risk of collision existed'. The definition 'aircraft' covers pretty well everything that flies and we get reports from all classes of aviators, from 747 captains to GA pilots, to gliders, hang gliders, microlite operators, parascenders and even parachutists. The objects they report are not only such conventional types but also balloons (some children's size), radio sondes, model aircraft and even recently an unidentified kite-like object over the North Sea. Now you will notice that I said 'when in the opinion of a pilot' and we cannot act on reports from ATC controllers, ground witnesses, MPs and so on, although quite a few get in touch with us. Those, like controllers who are in a position to judge proximity, if not

	A	AIRMISS REPORT
1 Name of pilot in command	B	1
2 Flight deck crew complement		2
Operator – include address and telephone no.	C	
Aircraft registration and type	D	
Colour scheme	E	HISLs ON/OFF*
1 Radio call sign		1
2 In communication with	F	2
3 Frequency		3
4 SSR Code		4 Mode C ON/OFF*
Aerodrome of departure	G	
Aerodrome of first intended landing	H	
Type of flight plan	I	*IFR/VFR/None CANP Filed YES/NO*
1 Position of Airmiss		1
2 Aircraft heading	J	2 *True/Magnetic
3 True airspeed		3 knots
1 Flight level, Altitude or Height		1 *FL .... / .... ft
2 Altimeter setting		2 .... mb (*standard/Reg, QNH/QNH/QFE)
3 Aircraft attitude	K	3 *Level/Climbing/Descending/Turning (*Right/Left)
4 Phase of flight		4 *Take-off En route descent Circuit
		Initial climb Holding Overshoot
		En route climb Final descent Aerobatics
		Cruise Landing Trg or Mil manoeuvres
Flight weather conditions at time of Airmiss	L	1 *IMC/VMC
		2 Distance .... ft *Above/Below *Cloud/Fog/Haze
		3 Distance .... *km/NM horizontally from cloud
		4 In *Rain/Snow/Sleet/Fog/Haze/Cloud/Between layers
		5 Flying *Into/out of sun
		6 Flight visibility .... *km/NM
		7 *Day/Night/Twilight
DATE and TIME (GMT) of Airmiss	M	Date: Time (GMT/UTC):
Description of other aircraft if relevant:		
1 Type, high/low wing, number of engines		1
2 Radio call sign, registration	N	2
3 Markings, colour, lighting		3
4 Other available details		4
1 Type of ATC service		1
2 First sighting distance		2
3 Horizontal and Vertical separation at time of Airmiss		3
4 Form of avoiding action taken If none, state reason	O	4
5 Assessment of risk of collision		5
6 Other relevant factors, i.e. workload, emergencies, vision from cockpit etc.		6

Whether Airmiss reported by radio, telephone or teleprinter. If yes state to which ATS Unit	P	*NO/YES BY RADIO (FREQ) PHONE/TELEPRINTER TO
Nature of Flight	Q	1 *PUBLIC TRANSPORT (Carriage for hire or reward)
		(a) Scheduled Passenger (b) Non-scheduled Passenger
		(c) Scheduled Freight (d) Non-scheduled Freight
		2 *COMMERCIAL 3 *EXECUTIVE 4 *CLUB GROUP
		5 *PRIVATE 6 *TRAINING 7 *GLIDING

DIAGRAMS OF AIRMISS

Mark passage of other aircraft relative to you, in plan on the left and in elevation on the right, assuming YOU are at the centre of each diagram.

VIEW FROM ABOVE   VIEW FROM ASTERN

DESCRIPTION OF AIRMISS

Include any details you think relevant or which will help the Joint Airmiss Working Group to understand what happened.

Continue over page if necessary

Date .... Time .... Signature of Pilot ....
of completion of form
Contact Tel. No.
*Delete and/or insert words or figures as appropriate   or Address ....

The CAA's form CA1094 'Airmiss Report – Pilot' which is filled in by every pilot who wishes to report that an incident has occurred whereby, in his opinion, 'his aircraft may have been endangered during flight by the proximity of another aircraft . . .'. (Courtesy CAA)

collision, risk have other forms of report. Ground witnesses may be helpful if they are talking about an actual airmiss already reported by the pilot – but, sadly, they rarely are. The fact of starting with a pilot-submitted report steers a lot of our subsequent procedure, as you will probably notice.

Now, why do we investigate these airmisses? There is only one reason – flight safety. An airmiss can be described as a near collision – some countries use that term – and if one investigates it and derives the available lessons from it, these lessons may be applied to hopefully prevent close encounters in similar circumstances, and any of such encounters might have ended in a collision. I said there was only one reason, and, if asked if there could be more, would certainly say that the second and third reasons were also 'flight safety' but there is perhaps some justification for saying that if one examines the trends of airmiss statistics over a number of years they will give a measure of guidance as to the health of the airspace under consideration in safety terms. A measure of guidance only, I emphasise, because one has to be pretty cautious about the use of these sort of statistics.

In the UK we have been in the airmiss business for a long time. Over 20 years ago we had two separate systems, with separate assessment groups for civil and military airmisses. Both were based at Uxbridge and run by the officials of the civil and military air traffic staffs at Hillingdon House. They chaired the separate assessment groups known respectively as the Civil and the Military Airmiss Working Group – the CAWG and the MAWG. In 1970 it was decided to set up a permanent unit, the joint airmiss section manned by personnel from the CAA and from MOD, to act as secretariat to the CAWG and MAWG. My predecessor, as the first OC JAS, then became the Chairman of both these groups. By this a great measure of commonality was established for the investigation of all airmisses in the UK FIR. This status lasted until 1977 when the 49 commonsense step was taken to amalgamate the two groups into one, the joint airmiss working group, with JAS as its secretariat and OC JAS as the chairman. This position has lasted to this day and we are, as far as I know, the only country in the world with a totally integrated civil and military system for airmiss investigation. In my opinion this is a huge advantage since civil and military aircraft share the airspace and to solve problems shown up by airmisses often needs joint civil and military action. As you can see from this, our organisation has evolved over a long period with the changes being derived by the interests of flight safety in a considered timescale. It is still evolving but it *is important that in these times of pressures from interests not solely dedicated to flight safety we do not permit changes to be made without time for full consideration of all their implications* [My italics, D.O.].

It is worth recalling that, while our system was evolving, ICAO [International Civil Aviation Organisation] laid down guidelines for an airmiss investigation system. I must admit to not knowing whether in fact we predated them, in which case, the guidelines may well have used the UK as a model, but in any case we now generally follow the ICAO system and I will indicate as we go along particular aspects where ICAO points the way.

Before we get into the nuts and bolts of reporting I should perhaps make clear my position as OC JAS in the national hierarchy. Like all my predecessors I am a serving RAF officer of the general duties, flying branch. JAS is a joint MOD/CAA organisation and my two executives are a civil ATCO [Air Traffic Control Officer] and an RAF squadron leader (also a pilot). We are supported by three other admin and clerical staff, two CAA and one RAF. We thus, like most of the units in the NATS organisation, are joint in make-up. However, my position is slightly unusual in that I do not have a simple chain of command. We are based at Uxbridge and co-located with the field HQ of NATS which is extremely convenient from a number of angles. JAS gets most of its admin and support services from field headquarters and for administrative matters and for operational advice I report to the Joint Field Commander (JFC) of the National Air Traffic Service. He is a civil CAA officer who heads a joint set-up with, under him, the director CATO and the AOC MATO. However, I can bypass this level and am policy adviser on airmiss matters to JFC's boss, that is the controller NATS, so I have direct access to him and his deputy. Beyond that I, like my predecessors, report direct and in person on airmiss matters to the Air Traffic Control Board at its annual meeting chaired jointly by the chairman CAA and CAS. Recently, it has also been decided that I will submit reports on airmisses and airmiss recommendations direct to these two extremely senior officials in their offices of joint chairmen of the ATC board. In practice this is all much less complicated than it seems and in my experience the outcome is that *I am able to be almost totally independent which is in my view what is needed for the proper conduct of the job* [My italics, D.O.]. Independence is also something which ICAO recommends.

So we come to the actual reporting of an airmiss. This clearly starts with the pilot and, once he has determined that in his opinion the incident he has just experienced qualifies as an airmiss he should, if he has a radio, tell an ATC unit without delay. If he cannot do this then he notifies it by phone as soon as he lands; this can be to an ATC unit or direct to a section at LATCC West Drayton called Aeronautical Information Section (Military) or AIS(MIL) for short. The ATC unit will also notify them by phone or telex. This is vital because AIS(MIL) will at once start tracing the other aircraft if its identity cannot be established by the local ATC unit. Here, of course, speed is vital because it may be possible to track down a 'Piper-type aircraft' an hour or even a day later but if the trail has had a week to go cold then it is a different matter. This is the sort of delay which happens if the immediate report has been omitted and the first we hear of the incident is the written report on the form CA1094 which should appear within a week. Incidentally this proforma is our amplification of the rather basic ICAO form. The AIS(MIL) staff do their best in either case, phoning all the possible clubs and operators. Following one clue to another and often making 70 or 80 phone calls over several weeks before succeeding or giving up the task is impossible. This happens in about 7 per cent of cases, almost always after late reports. Incidentally, radar recordings may greatly assist in tracing, even in the open FIR down to a few hundred feet, but it is limited since many of the lighter aircraft do

not paint well on radar and do not carry transponders [a device which makes the aircraft more visible to radar]. If the reported aircraft is foreign there is not much problem if it is military or a commercial on airways, but getting a response from club aircraft is much more difficult and falls to my staff who have to badger embassies, attachés, civil aviation authorities and so-on. Incidentally, our military reporting system is not very different from the civil one in that we get early notification by signal, followed up by written report which gets commented on by the flight safety staff at service HQs.

Once the other aircraft is traced its pilot should also submit a report. For commercial pilots of aircraft over 2300 kg this is not normally a problem since the Air Navigation Order requires them to fill in the form when we ask, and in any case they are professionals who see the value of it. There is sometimes more problem with general aviation and sport pilots where we depend on their goodwill. The great majority are responsible and comply at once but a minority are totally intransigent and refuse to fill in any report. Besides the loss of flight safety data it is inevitable that their failure to respond will lead the assessing group to consider that any failure is more likely to lie with them.

So now we know that an airmiss has taken place, have at least an initial pilot's report and can start the investigation. Here I must point out that an airmiss is not like an accident. There is no solid initial fact like a crashed aircraft to start with, indeed the whole edifice is built on a subjective basis, and one finds that there is not much hard evidence in the majority of cases. Even radar recordings, with the exception of height readouts from SSR [secondary surveillance radar], are not of much help when one is trying to decide exactly how close two aircraft came together when it is a matter of differentiating between, say, one and four hundred metres. So the investigation and later assessment must be suited to this basic condition. My staff raise a file for each airmiss. This starts with the pilots' reports and with both of these in hand there is usually a lot of phoning to resolve discrepancies in all manner of parameters. Naturally a fleeting incident leaves different and often incomplete impressions on minds variously influenced by fear, anger, indignation or guilt to mention only some of the factors. The outcome of such phone calls are recorded on the file. In due course we get transcripts of radio recordings and photos from the radar video recordings, where these are appropriate, and we can view radar replays where this can help an understanding of the geometry of the incident. However, detailed investigation into the ATC aspects of an incident are conducted for us by specialist staffs in the HQs of CATO and MATO, who conduct face-to-face interviews where necessary, assess all the recorded evidence and finally submit a collated report on control matters. These reports are also very useful in helping to establish the geometry of the incident where the pilot's reports are not clear. But I must emphasise here that by no means all, in fact the minority, of airmisses involve ATC even to the extent of an advisory service in uncontrolled airspace. Anyway, the files build up and descrepancies are, hopefully, resolved to our satisfaction to a point where I agree with my staff that we either have enough information for an assessment or, at the worst, have all we are going to get. At that stage it is drawn together into the initial part of the airmiss report ready for assessment.

Here we come back to the ICAO guidelines which say that an independent group should be set up to assess airmisses. The composition of ours has evolved over the years to what is shown here.

Joint Airmiss Working Group Membership

OC Joint Airmiss Section (Chairman)
British Airways
British Airlines Pilots Association
Guild of Air Pilots and Air Navigators
General Aviation Safety Committee
International Air Transport Association
British Helicopter Advisory Board
MOD Inspectorate of Flight Safety

MOD (PE)
RAF HQ Strike Command
RAF HQ Support Command
Royal Navy Air Command
Army Air Corps
USAF
Civil and RAF JAS Secretaries

It covers nominees from a wide range of aviation groups who between them ensure that the joint airmiss working group (the JAWG) has expertise from a broad spectrum of airspace users. The preponderance of pilot interests is important because *to get under the skin of an airmiss as reported by the pilots, usually subjectively, requires the sort of feeling that can only be gained in a cockpit* [My italics D.O.].

One gets the feel for the factors like fright or indignation which can bias a report and one can often get a good feel for what may have been left out. The range of experience in the group is important because we can usually turn to someone with experience on, or at least knowledge of, the aircraft in question or who has flown in the airspace we are discussing. We already have a good deal of air traffic advice round the table, there are invariably the civil and military incident investigators and I suppose at most meetings there are five or six controllers present. However, the question of further ATC nominees is being discussed at present. I should emphasise here that the JAWG members act as experts dedicated to flight safety and not as factional representatives who will support 'their man' right or wrong. Indeed it is usual for the specialist in a particular area to highlight the faults shown up in his specialisation because he appreciates them better than anyone else. The group meets once a month and we aim to follow the ICAO directive shown below.

ICAO GUIDELINES FOR AIRMISS ASSESSMENT
Terms of Reference for Working Group

1. Determine the Cause (Do not allocate blame)
2. Assess Risk of Collision
   A Actual Risk of Collision
   B Possible Risk of Collision
   C No Risk of Collision
   D Risk not Determined
3. Formulate Recommendations
4. Analyse by categories, locations, etc and highlight trends
   and
   Take follow-up action
   Inform all those directly involved
   Publish matters of general interest
   Preserve anonymity

Primarily we have to determine the cause, but not (as ICAO says) allocate blame. Of course, if we say the cause rests with the failure of an individual, others may imply blame to him. But we do not. We also have no part to play in any regulatory or legal process. Other specialists deal with the civil and military aspects of these matters, whether they involve pilots or controllers. We keep the airmiss system entirely separate from them and for this reason all reports put to the JAWG are made anonymous by having names of individuals and companies excluded. Anonymity is another ICAO requirement. Then, as ICAO says, the group has to assess the risk of collision and here too we follow their guidelines although in the UK we do not actually use a **D**; if the evidence is insufficient to select a risk level, we just call it unassessable. We also follow ICAO in the matter of recommendations and analysis of data, but I think these points can be brought out best if I lead you through the whole process of presenting an airmiss to the JAWG and what comes after.

A week before each meeting we circulate an agenda with the partly completed reports for all the airmisses we hope to discuss; this gives members a chance to read themselves in, which is vital for the more complicated cases. On the day there are perhaps 20 – 25 persons round the table. Each case is presented by the JAS executive who has handled the file and he will have prepared a Vu-foil showing the location and flightpaths involved, as best we can interpret them. He will read out the airmiss report to reinforce members' preparatory reading. Then the case is opened for general discussion. This can take from perhaps five minutes for a simple cut-and-dried case to well over an hour for a really complicated one perhaps involving several control agencies and different classes of airspace. In one like that we usually need extra explanations by the ATC investigator and the expertise of members familiar with the aircraft type or that particular airspace area is always helpful. In the end, when all the members have a fairly clear agreement on what happened we come to decide on the cause. This may itself be the subject of discussion and may be split between two or more factors either on an equal basis or with some contributing to others. On occasion differences cannot be resolved by discussion and then I call on the members to vote and the majority view prevails. I have a casting vote but in over two years have only, I think, had to exercise it once. We then do much the same for the risk, again voting if necessary. I should emphasise here that the risk that is allocated is based on the passage of the two aircraft as it actually transpired. We cannot base it on 'if the other pilot had not seen me . . .' or 'in cloud this would have been dangerous . . .'. So it is actual risk, not potential risk. Also the risk does not necessarily reflect the seriousness with which the JAWG views the incident. An airmiss involving some appalling lapse of airmanship or where there has been a gross error by a controller may end with the aircraft passing a safe distance apart even if it is less than regulation requires, so it is classified **C**. In cases where there is some serious matter which if not corrected could lead to a similar airmiss, or worse, to a collision the JAWG will raise a recommendation. This can be directed to any aspect, flying or aircraft control, and is usually phrased to highlight the problem that needs correction but not normally specifying what corrective action is to be taken. For lesser matters or to reinforce some corrective action already being taken as the result of an airmiss the group may register a formal comment. It is only a small minority of cases which justify recommendation or comment. At the end of a hard day's work the JAWG will have got through 20-25 cases.

After the meeting my executives will write up a summary of the discussion, which will always highlight flight safety aspects thrown up by each case. The write-up will make it clear where there have been differences of opinion within the group and where a majority decision has been reached. The airmiss report is completed with statements of risk, cause and, where appropriate, the recommendation or comment. About a week after the meeting copies of this completed report will go to the pilots, controlling units and everyone else involved in the actual incident. At the same time I will send a compilation of the meeting's air misses to the two chairmen of the ATC board. We then have another important task, which again follows ICAO guidance. This is to code each airmiss under some 70 data parameters which are recorded on a computer input sheet and then input to our data base. This holds information on all airmisses back for some 20 years and enables us to examine trends, indicate geographical black spots and so on, which can reinforce a recommendation or call for remedial action on their own account. It is, of course, also useful in answering a variety of questions including those from MPs.

Last of the immediate actions, I will raise a formal letter to present any recommendation or serious comment. This will be directed to the chairman CAA or CAS, as appropriate, but copies will go direct to the authorities, civil or military, who will have to implement the recommendation. I would normally direct this at two-star level in a military context or its equivalent in the civil world. In my experience these are invariably taken seriously and in due course I always receive a statement of action taken. This is reported back to the JAWG.

Normally we will deal with a case some three to four months after it is reported. Occasionally it takes less but sometimes it can take up to six months for all the reports to come to us. This compares well with other countries; many in Europe take over a year, while the American FAA's target is 90 days, but they at times take over six months.

Every four months we publish three compilations of airmiss reports and statistics. The first of these has a considerable spread of detailed airmiss statistics and copies of all the airmisses reported in the four month period. It goes to a wide official-use-only circulation of bodies involved with operating or controlling aircraft who have a direct influence on flight safety. The circulation has always been limited because we are concerned that too much publicity, even with anonymity, could lead to a reduction in reporting rate or of 53 reporting detail. As I said earlier, commercial pilots are required to report under the ANO but we depend on the goodwill of pilots of other cases. There has always been a worry that a pilot either may not report at all or that he will prune the report of anything that might show him in a bad light – and this would cut the JAWG off from important information and stop us passing on the lesson to others.

The next document we produce is a compilation of all airmisses involving controller error. This has a foreword written by the joint field commander of NATS which highlights lessons and points of interest appropriate to his air traffic controller readers. This goes on an official circulation to all air traffic units in the country.

Finally, we produce a booklet with seven selected airmisses involving general aviation aircraft, usually chosen so that they bring out strong flight safety lessons often with a common theme or themes. I write a foreword to this emphasising these flight safety points. The book goes out to flying clubs and schools, being circulated with the general aviation safety information leaflet (the GASIL) and is also on public sale.

One last, newer publication, has been put out by the CAA (not by us) for just over a year. This gives a breakdown of airmiss statistics and in particular those involving commercial air transport aircraft. The chairman of the CAA has decided that from the issue just published this will also include the full text of all airmiss reports involving these commercial aircraft. This book is distributed widely by the CAA and is on public sale.

Incidentally, even before this change we were, as far as I am aware, by far the most open country in Europe when it comes to releasing details of airmiss reports. USA, with its Freedom of Information Act, is of course more open but I gather that those who have an active part to play in improving flight safety do not always find this an advantage.

I think I have now covered the outline of the reporting, investigating and follow-up of airmisses. It might be useful now to give an outline of statistics – *how the airmiss scene really is and not how you read about it in the popular press* [My italics, D.O.].

First, I think it is important to set the broad picture as shown below.

Airmisses in UK FIR
1.   About 150-200 airmiss reports are filed each year.
2.   About 40% assessed as involving some collision risk ie, **A** or **B**.
3.   About 8% assessed as definite collision risk ie, **A**.
4.   Most occur below 3,000 ft.
5.   Over 80% reported in VMC.
6.   Over 50% occur in open FIR.
7.   The majority – 70% – are due to human failing. Few are due to technical failure.

The JAWG deals with, on average, 170 or so airmisses per year, though in the last few years, as in the early 1970s, the numbers are higher. The figure of 40 per cent assessed as being **A** or **B**, that is risk-bearing, is a pretty consistent one, varying only a few percentage points from year to year. The 8 per cent of risk-bearing – the 'Oh my God!' incidents – is also pretty consistent though, being a smaller statistical sample, it is subject to more random variation. In any case, as you will have seen the differentation between **A** and **B** is fairly subjective – on the whole I suppose the swings and roundabouts of risk assessment balance out. The next figures may come as a surprise; the vast majority of airmisses do not involve commercial aircraft in regulated airspace. Most, well over 70 per cent, take place in the lower airspace and the majority in the open FIR. Even of those in regulated airspace, quite a number will be in the aerodrome traffic zones of small airfields and often caused by infringements of the zones or by poor airmanship in the circuit. It might not seem surprising that most happen in VMC, since the report requires the pilot to assess that a risk exists and in cloud he may not even be aware of the other aircraft. But we do get some filed in cloud, many more in intermittent IMC and a number at night.

A minority it is true, but of course there is much less recreational flying and less military low flying at night. Lastly, and not surprising, most airmisses are caused by human failing, and of these about three times as many are caused by pilots as by

controllers. *The main failure here is weaknesses in lookout, either because the pilot just fails to see*

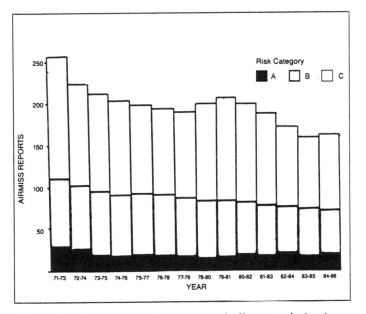

Chart showing 3-year moving average of all reported airmisses.

the other aircraft or because he is distracted by cockpit activity. There is no doubt that lookout is the key to survival whenever one flies [My italics, D.O.]. The other side of that is that anything that can be done to enhance aircraft conspicuity is a good thing. Pilots too often show lack of consideration, particularly if they are in a fast aircraft passing something smaller and less manoeuverable. They know they will clear by a distance which eliminates all risk of collision but the other chap, taken by surprise, gets his adrenalin well stirred up and justifiably files an airmiss. The faster aircraft is by no means always a military pilot.

Turning to the annual figures, the accompanying chart shows how airmiss totals, with the **A**, **B** and **C** proportions indicated, have altered through the years.

The pillars represent three-year moving averages which smooths out the random deviations and shows a generally decreasing tendency until the final pillar and I have indicated that 1987 continues this recent upward trend, although we have not finished assessing the risk breakdown. However, it is interesting to find when one digs into the statistics that the recent increases are almost entirely made up of airmisses in the lower airspace, in open FIR. *My own opinion is that what we are experiencing is a higher rate of reporting, perhaps more of the iceberg being revealed than an increase in actual conflictions. Over the past 18 months it has been very noticeable that in a month where airmisses have featured frequently on telly or the front pages, the number of airmisses reported is markedly up when compared with the same month in previous years* [My italics, D.O.]. So I think this high media profile plays a part in making someone who has had a closeish encounter think that it was an 'airmiss' and he had better find out what to do with it. Also a staff officer from HQ MATO has been visiting a wide range of flying clubs and among other things has been advertising our work, explaining the airmiss system and encouraging its proper use. We aim at a higher reporting rate even if it increases the apparent number of airmisses, since we then increase our database and chance of improving flight safety.

To move on to the airmisses involving commercial air transport aircraft, fixed wing and rotary, I thought I would present figures in a raw annual form so that there can be no suggestion of juggling by using a three-year moving average.

On the lower line I have plotted the rate of CAT involvement in risk-bearing (A and B) airmisses per 100,000 flying hours. I use this figure since it is one the CAA often quotes. 55

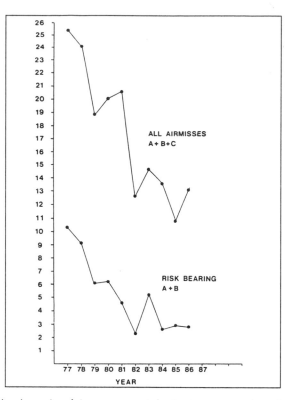

Graph showing airmisses involving commercial air transport aircraft, (fixed wing and rotary) per 100,000 hours flying.

You can see that although there is a good deal of random fluctuation *there is a steady underlying downward curve* [My italics, D.O.]. However, I earlier said to you that the risk bearing assessment could include a measure of luck, so I plotted the figure for CAT aircraft in all airmisses in the top line. Again, allowing for random variations the downward trend is marked. I don't suppose that whatever one does and whatever new systems come in one can ever eliminate human error so that probably the curves will inevitably flatten out, but it will be interesting to see what happens when functions like 'short term conflict alert' are introduced to the air traffic system. It seems to me, that when one considers these statistics one must conclude that *some of the statements on the number of airmisses have been based on very shaky ground* [My italics, D.O.].

In the end, do I think it is all worthwhile? The answer is a definite yes. I am convinced that we have a system for airmiss investigation which certainly sets the standard for Europe and probably for the world. The JAWG is remarkably independent and certainly makes its recommendations without fear or favour. One we made a year or so back got some publicity in the aviation press. There were a series of airmisses in 1986 where hang-gliders and low-flying military jets got much too close together. The hang-gliders are notoriously difficult to see and their views of the front end of the jets were much too close. I recall comments like 'I don't know what it was but it had a lot of rivets . . . .', and 'I was looking down its intakes and shut my eyes . . . It missed me but I don't know how the other pilot managed it'. The JAWG believed that if the situation continued someone would be killed and we raised a recommendation that action should be taken to integrate the operations of these two classes of airspace users. I did not get many thanks from my masters for raising an apparently insoluble problem but representatives from the two sides got together under the chairmanship of a NATS official and with considerable give and take thrashed out a system by which the hang-gliders nominated 30-odd primary sites for weekday use which the military agreed they would avoid. This was trialled through 1987 and it may have been luck but there were only four hang-gliders/military airmisses in 1987, and two of these were due to missplotting of sites on maps. I trust that now the system has become permanent the level will remain low. This is one simple instance of the beneficial effect of the JAWG. It does point up our sole aim – the enhancement of flight safety.

As an arm of NATS – and someone said recently that perhaps it is the healthiest arm – the Joint Airmiss Working Group performs an excellent task and does so without the enforced constraints of political or commercial bias. It has a reputation for operating to the highest level of traditional British standards and without doubt it is the best airmiss investigation system in the world; certainly other nations are envious of its credibility and many endeavour to emulate its practices and procedures.

One of the most significant findings in the airmiss investigation process is that more than 50 per cent of all the incidents reported are through late sightings by the pilots concerned. This means that with improved lookout and prompt action, the majority of reported incidents would be avoided. Unfortunately this is a growing symptom resulting from excessive reliance on air traffic control as the source of all information. In earlier years all pilots – private and professional – were trained and became accustomed to rely on their own visual judgement and making their own decisions on any action that might be necessary. This quality of good, sound airmanship is one that has been seriously eroded as people have become increasingly reliant on the outside help that has become available. As mentioned elsewhere in the book, there are many occasions on which pilots are not sure of the level of air traffic service that they are receiving and sometimes they feel that because they are speaking to a controller, they are entirely in his hands. Merely being in communication with a controller does not alter the fact that the commander of any aircraft is responsible for the safe conduct of his machine. My fears are shared; I quote: 'I am concerned about the current trends in air traffic control. It is my opinion that the ability of a pilot to take-off and fly . . . is threatened by controllers assuming a role that is not theirs, with pilots being encouraged to depend on ATCOs outside controlled airspace.'. . . . 'Controllers are also taking it upon themselves to separate VFR aircraft, inside and outside controlled airspace which again takes the onus away from the pilot.' The letter from which this was quoted was written not by a pilot but by a controller at a major airport who, not surprisingly, asks to be in the anonymous category mentioned at the start of the book. Coming from someone in the front line of the subject it brings home the point more meaningfully than my words can do.

An aspect that has received little attention in assessing the standard of lookout among pilots concerns the contents of the cockpit. Two aircraft of the same type, equipped to markedly different standards of instrumentation, can produce equally different styles of operation. Here Bill Wainwright, a test pilot with British Aerospace, explains:

The effect that a modern flight deck has on the way we fly an aircraft was brought home to me vividly in 1987 when I flew two BAe 125-800 aircraft on identical sorties on consecutive days. Both were destined to be Company demonstrators, and I had to assess their stalling characteristics in short flights out of Hatfield, over East Anglia, and then back to base. One of the aircraft was remaining in Britain and was a fully completed machine with an Electronic Flight Instrument display (EFIS); the other was going to be our demonstrator in the USA and would be finished out there. It was only fitted with some very basic instruments for the ferry flight – a tiny artificial horizon of the kind that is fitted as a standby instrument in our BAe 146 and a simple compass system.

I flew the American demonstrator first and noticed that I was particularly alert as I flew outbound from Hatfield at a couple of thousand feet. I was proud of my instrument scan, which recalled memories of my days as an instructor on Jet Provosts many years before, as I flicked my attention rapidly between the primary attitude display and the other instruments. I then noticed that I was sharing this quick instrument scan with looking outside at the visual picture; I was using the real horizon to supplement the relatively poor information from my small artificial horizon, and because of this, my lookout was much better than usual.

When I flew the British demonstrator, with its glass cockpit, my immediate impression was of being more relaxed. The quality of information received from my EFIS display was so good that I had little need for anything else, and I could fly very accurately without looking outside! In fact, I noticed that my attention was constantly drawn back inside whenever I glanced outside by the pretty picture and wealth of detail on my EFIS attitude and navigation displays. I realised that I was playing with the options on my displays, and that there was far more information available than I required for the job in hand. I was spending very little time searching outside for other aircraft, but that didn't matter since I was being watched on radar by Air Traffic Control.

I am not a member of JAWG, but I feel that, wherever possible, it is right to gain front-seat knowledge of the subject on which I am writing, so as soon as I declared my intention to lay stress in this book on airmisses, I was very pleased to be invited by the Chairman to attend a meeting of the group. So, as a silent observer, on 15th February 1989 I visited the Joint Airmiss Section of NATS at Royal Air Force Uxbridge and heard a full day's very thorough investigation into the causes of recent incidents.

My discoveries on this occasion caused me to change nothing in my songs of praise for the group's working methods, except, perhaps, to strengthen the notes from *mezzo* to *forte*. In particular, I can confirm that some earlier misgivings expressed by politicians about either the constitution or the workings of JAWG are entirely unfounded. These are merely further examples of well-worn practices in which Members of Parliament shout from their party perches about subjects on which they have no working knowledge. In fact, the standard of professionalism expressed within the group could serve as a productive lesson to many other bodies, including the House of Commons. Most notably, each member is present to use his specific expertise for the benefit of UK flight safety as a whole and there is a total absence of bias in favour of a person's own patch.

Perhaps the most important aspect of all this is that an airmiss should be (and is) treated as a subject for serious study, in the hope that a way or ways may be found to reduce the likelihood of a recurrence. In a developed society the airmiss should not be material for emotive explosions and I must repeat that by its own nature it cannot be and cannot lead to an accident. Where we have gone wrong is not in the air, but on the ground where all the tales are assembled, exaggerated, embellished and regurgitated *ad nauseam*. Some of the sources of those sins are exposed in the chapter that follows.

Chapter 7
Who
Creates the Myths?

'I am not too worried how much you disagree among yourselves, but I am concerned that this should get out of professional hands and into the grip of politicians who have no knowledge of the subject.'
'Speak up. Be frank. We have taken especial care to ensure that there is no-one from the press here today.'

THESE ARE the gists of statements made by the Chairmen of two meetings of aviation working groups on which I have had the privilege to serve. That these points needed to be made reflects considerable discredit on substantial sections of the community, for in these words those who should speak and those who should publish the truth are placed squarely in the dock. Unfortunately, though, experience of the extent to which relatively minor incidents – or in some cases even non-incidents – have been expanded beyond reason leads people who need to examine a possible problem in a cold and logical way to exclude all whose motives may be suspect. An unfortunate need among some politicians to chase after vote-catching brownie points and vociferous greed among the lower echelons of the media to invent best-selling headlines combine to act as constraints on those who work genuinely towards seeking improvements in flight safety.

Let me begin by telling the 'true' tale – true only in that it was printed – published in the *Daily Mirror* during April 1988. Under a heading 'I SAW THE MIRACLE OF THE AIRMISS JETS' followed 'shocked witnesses tell of 1000 mph drama'. To provide this horror story a DC10 of American Airlines and an Aer Lingus Boeing 737 are alleged to have come close to each other over Strumble in South Wales. The witnesses who provided such valuable and unchallengeable detail to the *Mirror* were a woman hanging her washing in her garden in Gwent, which is 70 miles from where the machines passed each other, and another witness from rather further away, in Cardiff. We cannot expect to find aviation expertise among the members of the public who choose to contact the tabloids, but surely we can hope for some sense or reason to take precedence over sheer scandal before material is published in a paper that is inflicted on large sections of the nation? Apparently not.

Fortunately the CAA press office has the welcome habit of issuing news releases to counter the inaccuracies with which some sections of the press seem to 59 specialise, but usually the truth fails to qualify as news and once the trouble-causing scandal has appeared in print this is all that the general reader is allowed to know. The news that there was no news is unlikely to be popular material for a journalist, so the truth fails to be given a place. To show that the Authority tries hard to provide the public with the facts in a correct and calculated way I am pleased to be able to publish two examples of releases issued in response to incorrect and damaging information that the tabloid press insists on printing.

In the first case, adjacent to the bold caption 'TERRIFIED PLANE PASSENGER FILMS DRAMA AT 8000 FT' and next to a video-still photo the text read 'This is the terrifying moment when passengers froze in fear while Flight BR775 circled above Gatwick airport . . . .' The eye-witness reported that 'It felt at one stage that we were in touching distance.'

For the truth, read the accompanying news release from the CAA press office.

NEWS RELEASE

Civil Aviation Authority

CAA House, 45—59 Kingsway, London WC2B 6TE

---

29 April 1988

DAILY MIRROR "NEAR MISS" STORY

The Civil Aviation Authority has checked out the radar recordings for the two aircraft involved in the incident reported in today's Daily Mirror.

These recordings show that no airmiss took place. Neither pilot has filed an airmiss report and neither has any intention of doing so.

The 1,000 foot vertical separation referred to in the Daily Mirror article is the standard separation for aircraft in controlled airspace. The two aircraft were never closer than 1,000 feet.

Nothing unusual or unsafe took place.

41.88

PRESS OFFICE
Tel: 01-379 7311 extension 5335
Fax: 01-379 4784

CAA

The second incident that illustrates so well the level of accuracy in reporting in the national press was a case in which two aircraft were alleged in one paper to have come within half a mile of each other and in another the horizontal separation was quoted as three miles. The lower figure turned out to be inaccurate and the greater distance, which was nearer to the truth, should not have warranted any publicity. If we persuade the non-aviation public that aircraft are in dangerous situations when they have three miles of airspace between them, then we are guilty of creating alarm based on false values.

In the air the lack of background features, variable cloudscapes and lighting conditions, and lack of certainty of the actual size of the aircraft being viewed make distance judgement extremely difficult. Even with the help of background information can you tell how far the airborne 767 is from the nearest 727. In fact it is well over the 1000 ft that is the standard vertical separation for air transport operations. (Air Portraits copyright)

Aircraft sizes do vary enormously. In the background can be seen the Antonov An-124, at 405 metric tonnes weight and 240 ft wing span one of the World's greatest aircraft. The historic DH.88 Comet in the foreground is tiny in comparison; but they do share the same airspace. (Air Portraits copyright) 61

As a logical follow-on, vertical separation is an aspect that causes more confusion than horizontal distance; I recall two occasions on which I have heard people exclaim that two aeroplanes were about to collide. This is understandable, for variations in size can make height estimations difficult even for those of us with lifetimes in aviation, so we must expect people to see danger when none exists. There is no easy solution to this problem, but the thought of possible collision brought about by media publicity must be a significant factor in the amount of unjustified concern that wafts about. Shortly after the mid-air collisions to the Italian *Frecce Tricolori* in Germany in 1988, the RAF's Battle of Britain Memorial Flight was scheduled to do a flypast over a public park. I heard one man mention this to his wife, clearly in the hope that she would go with him, but she replied: 'After all I've been reading in the paper about the dangers, you won't get me standing anywhere near that lot.' Then I examined some of the over-dramatised reports that had appeared – some in papers that would have been expected to handle the situation more responsibly – and it became easy to understand why otherwise sound souls, who tend to *believe* what they read, or what they see on 'the box', become frightened through misinformation.

Unfortunately some discussions within our two Houses of Parliament create impressions that do more harm than good. Whilst I can muster no sympathy for the scandal-seeking press I can understand why some gross distortions of fact emanate from politicians. After all, with both his local and central commitments, a Member may be called upon to become involved in every subject from babies, social security, and road schemes to education problems, nuclear policy, shopping precincts, and defence. The problem seems to be that some MPs get themselves involved quite unnecessarily in subjects about which they know little and on which they like to pretend to be authorities. They could avoid public derision by choosing their subjects more selectively. I quote a few examples from Hansard, with my reactions in italic:

The time might be on the horizon when to go on having individual inquiries into airmisses should be replaced by an inquiry into the whole question of air traffic control to try to reassure the many who flew and the many who lived under the flight path.
If each airmiss is not investigated individually, how would an inquiry into ATC produce the answer? Anyhow, many airmisses do not involve air traffic control

The skies had become like the A74 road. They were too crowded. *See the truth in Chapter 12*

Re Heathrow:
It was alarming to live under the flight path.
Why? What comfort does this observation give to residents and what purpose does it serve?

What was a non-risk-bearing airmiss? If it was not a risk, why was it reported?
Perhaps that speaker will read the paper by the Chairman of the Joint Airmiss Working Group in Chapter 6

Was everything being done to encourage reporting [of airmisses] so that there were reliable statistics?

Every pilot is aware of the reporting procedure and, as a result of known encouragement to use it even with a marginal case, the majority of reported airmisses involve no collision risk

When Paul Channon, Secretary of State for Transport, explained that there had been a very good safety record and praised both pilots and controllers, the chief opposition spokesman on transport retorted that Mr Channon was becoming so complacent that he had degenerated into using claptrap.

In the middle of 1988 the CAA press office needed to issue a news release denying statements by certain MPs who laid blame on the Authority for air traffic disruption that had been caused entirely by problems of striking controllers abroad.

Even after the tragic accident at Lockerbie in December 1988, the reports in Hansard reflect little credit on some MPs who, interspersed with messages of sympathy for the sufferers and appreciation for the workers involved, indulged in some quite inappropriate political slanging contests.

Unfortunately the BBC, too, cannot claim a clean record. Again the CAA felt the need to issue a news release to counter a radio announcement that two aircraft had missed each other by only 100 feet. The BBC had omitted the relevant bit: that they were 2 - 3 miles apart horizontally.

Instead of allowing our judgement to be warped by the sins of the media and by the panics in Parliament, we should digest a few unchallengeable facts.

Firstly, in 1978, when the commercial air transport sector flew an estimated 440,000 hours, there were 31 risk-bearing airmisses involving 40 CAT aircraft, producing 9.1 such machines reported in risk-bearing incidents in each 100,000 hours flown. Ten years later, by which the total hours were estimated as 606,000, there were 11 airmisses involving 13 CAT aircraft, or 2.1 for each 100,000 hours. The papers were not filled with airmiss reports when they were relatively common, but by their very rarity they have become news for those who seek to gain something from their dramatic journalism. Perhaps this is comparable with the situation on the roads, for while we continue to kill each other at the rate of roughly 16 people each day we see relatively little mention in the media, but if the Department of Transport succeeds in making our roads much safer, then perhaps we shall see the happy time in which the occasional accident will qualify as a headline hitter? Certainly it would be comforting to reach such a state of security.

Perhaps now I can hear you asking how there can be 11 airmisses involving only 13 aircraft, as, you say rightly, two machines must be present to create an incident. Here, however, we are considering only aircraft in which fare-paying passengers were being carried, but an incident can concern machines in any category, eg private aeroplane to military jet, airliner to civil helicopter and so on.

When there is some good news to pass to the public, such as a marked reduction in the number of airmisses, the varying treatment given by different sections of the press may prove of interest. Top marks here go to the *Daily Express*:

'Safest Summer ever in the sky

The skies over Britain had their safest spell on record last summer. The CAA says that from May to the end of August there were only two airmisses involving commercial flights. Neither was classified as "a definite risk" . . . .'

But now to the *Daily Mirror* again:

'48 jets in near misses

About 50 planes were involved in near misses over Britain in the peak holiday season last year, it was disclosed yesterday . . . .'

In case you feel that they must have been reporting different stories, I should add that both were published on 4th May 1988. The sad part of the story is that both tales are true. There *were* 48 reported airmisses, but only two were assessed as being marginally serious. It depends on what message you wish to portray to your readership: the significance of the truth or a spot of eye-catching drama.

Another occasion on which the CAA found cause to issue a press release was when a Concorde carried out a go-around because the captain, who is responsible for the safety of his aircraft and passengers, wisely decided to do so because another aircraft ahead was being slow in clearing the far end of the runway. There was no danger and a missed approach is not an uncommon occurrence. However, *Today* for 23rd May 1988 printed the bold headline 'CONCORDE YARDS FROM CRASH' and the *Daily Mirror* for the same day competed in the race with

---

NEWS RELEASE

Civil Aviation Authority

CAA House, 45 — 59 Kingsway, London WC2B 6TE

---

23 May 1988

CONCORDE `GO-AROUND`

The circumstances of Friday's Concorde landing at Heathrow have been confirmed as routine and no inquiry is called for. The Civil Aviation Authority said today passengers were in no danger.

The go-around, or missed approach, is itself a safety measure at all airports. It is clearly laid down in Heathrow Airport's published procedures for pilots and is a requirement of the International Civil Aviation Organisation.

Heathrow's two runways have a planned capacity of 72 take offs and landings per hour. This high rate of runway utilisation sometimes means that if an aircraft is slow to clear the runway, the aircraft following it in to land needs to go around and come in again.

Modern jet aircraft have the capability to come in exceedingly low before the pilot needs to decide to go ahead or miss his approach. Aircraft with the most up-to-date technology can come down to a height of only 12 feet before this decision needs to be made.

48.88

PRESS OFFICE.
Tel: 01-379 7311 extension 335
Fax: 01-379 4784

CAA

'RUNWAY SCARE FOR CONCORDE'. Perhaps the CAA release could have included the adage oft-used in flying circles that 'every approach is an approach to a go-around, but if everything is in order, then a pilot can afford to convert that approach to a landing'.

I have tried hard to find some substance to the growing concern about mid-air safety. I have failed. Airmisses, of course, will continue to occur and will continue to be over-reported, for there is no way in which an absolute guarantee can be given that no two aeroplanes will come within sight of each other; but even this, harmless in itself, is a subjective matter, for what one pilot considers to be a safe clearance may worry another who takes it upon himself to file an 'Airmiss Report'. But even this is not a bad move, for the more genuine incidents that go through the investigation process the greater is the total of amassed knowledge of the subject. It is one matter, however, for a pilot to make a report so that his siting can be researched and the findings recorded, to be unearthed later in the continual search for improvement, but it is beneficial to no-one for the *Daily Mirror* or any other paper to splash 'Shocked witnesses tell of 1000 mph drama' at an unguarded readership.

Times and attitudes, of course, change. To add weight to my point, there are no true stories of recent *serious* incidents over the UK, but I can find *one* relating to a British airliner. Even for one, however, we need to turn back the pages of history for 35 years and go to French airspace to find it. On 11th August 1954 an Airspeed Ambassador of British European Airways (known by that organisation as the Elizabethan class) was descending in cloud to Paris Le Bourget, when, to quote the pilot, 'a grey mass shot past the windscreen. The engines of another aircraft roared briefly and it was gone'. In fact, the Ambassador and the other aircraft, a DC-4 of Air France, made physical contact in the air and immediately after the incident the French captain said on the radio 'That was a beet close, eh? We must 'ave a beer sometime'. On landing the British and French aircraft were seen to have a dangling wingtip and one buckled propeller respectively. The pilot of the Ambassador was the late Ron Gillman, with whom I was well acquainted at the time. Although clearly shaken, his attitude to his mid-air experience was typical of the time: that just because it had happened once – and everyone had survived safely anyway – this did not mean that there was a likelihood of it occurring again. This reflects a pertinent point, for human lives then were just as valuable as they are today, but perhaps because we had a major war only a few years behind us we had no need to burst into hysterics after an incident in which no-one was killed or even injured. Certainly today's practice of carrying out a thorough investigation into each reported incident is a move to be applauded, but the near-panics shouted in the Commons and strewn across front pages of the papers are trends to be despised.

I am very pleased – as you should be – that there is such a shortage of tales to tell about mid-air collisions. There appears to have been only one case in the whole of aviation history in which a British-registered airliner made in-flight contact with another aircraft in British airspace: a BEA Dakota and an Anson of the RAF near Coventry in February 1949 – sustantially more than 40 years ago.

So perhaps I should complete this chapter with some words from Keith Mack, speaking to the Aerodrome Owners Association in September 1988, when he was Controller of NATS: 'Despite the efforts of the media to portray our industry at every opportunity as one which provides a regular source of shock, horror and chaos, more people have been safely transported to and from UK airports than ever before in the history of aviation'.

Chapter 8
Other Risks

ALTHOUGH AIRMISSES form the centre of gravity in terms of public concern over flight safety, this is because they provide good, dramatic material for the media and make stories that are readily readable; but if we wish to take safety seriously we need to delve more deeply and get away from the headline hitters. I am not denying that airmisses are causes for concern, for the work carried out by the Joint Airmiss Section of NATS and the associated Joint Airmiss Working Group must be among the most significant of all in the overall search for safety. No airmiss has ever hurt anyone, however, but there are numerous other problems that cannot claim such immunity.

Experience proves that aircraft are inherently safe. They must be properly designed, built and maintained, as must their engines and all the increasingly complex array of equipment with which they are fitted. Aerodromes used for most revenue-earning operations must be licensed. Organisations operating commercially must hold air operators' certificates. There is a protective air traffic control system. Pilots and relevant engineers must be appropriately licensed. There are limits on times between airframe, engine and component ovehauls and pilots have laid-down flight-time limitations. All this shows that aviation is more heavily monitored than any other form of travel and it is right that this should be the case; for although, when properly conducted, flying shares top place for safety, the potential for accident resulting from error in any quarter is high.

The major accidents at Lockerbie in Scotland in December 1988 and on the M1 on the approach to East Midlands Airport in January 1989 brought the whole subject of safety to the fore; and here we have positive examples of two entirely different ways in which loopholes can break through the regulatory system. One *could* be lack of care and concern over security at an airport and the other *might* be traced back to faults in the manufacturing process; but still many months will pass before final reports are published and we must all take extreme care not to pass our own judgement before the facts are confirmed. Accident investigation is a lengthy, painstaking and complex process and only if such detailed procedure is followed can the results be accepted with credibility. Anyone who has seen the workings of the Department of Transport Air Accidents Investigation Branch (AAIB) at Farnborough will appreciate the extent of the trouble that is taken to establish cause. In the hangar are sections in which all the available parts of a crashed aircraft are brought together and as far as is possible remated, for often the parts that cannot be found provide the key to the case.

Although, to those who suffer in any way in or as the result of an accident, knowledge of the cause of the occurrence cannot soften the blow, I should make the point that, whatever the findings, neither at Lockerbie nor at East Midlands will the reason be found to be in any way related to the *primary* subject of this book. Very tragic though they were, they were not associated with airspace design or management and they do not influence any results that we may reach concerning this subject, but they have revealed something that seems to be significant in terms of public awareness: that in general (although as always we can find the exception) the reporting of these fatal accidents has been factually more correct than is the case with the average and relatively harmless airmiss. A search through the headlines shows that even after these two serious mishaps, cases in which aircraft *may* have flown too close to each other for someone's peace of mind have been the subject of greater drama than have the reportings of the two real accidents. In these latter cases, perhaps the biggest journalistic sins have been the tendencies for some to become self-appointed experts and report on mere possibilities as though they were proven facts. This can be very damaging to the task of finding the truth; and nearly as harmful as the inexcusably thoughtless practice of removing items to hold as souvenirs.

Now we will look at some of the causes of hazards to the safety of flight. Throughout the world, 1007 people died in air accidents in 1988, but there were 1,100 million passenger journeys in the year, so this produces a mathematically convenient ratio of about one fatality for each million passengers carried. Pilot error accounted for the greatest number of accidents, followed by those that were weather-related, with outside influences such as action by terrorists taking a close third place. Although in this book we are concerned mainly with activities in and over the UK, we are in the fortunate position that we have so few accidents to record that any derived information would be statistically meaningless. Following the small-sample argument to its illogical limit, we could say that because one British-operated airliner crashed in Britain following engine problems, killing 47 people, the most likely cause of death in an air accident in the UK in a home-registered aeroplane is engine trouble. This, of course, is wholly unsustainable.

Because of its continuing pertinence in so many areas of activity – and not the least in aviation – security must be·near the top of any list for attention. With a long history of both hijacking and the planting of both explosive and incendiary devices on board airliners, terrorism may be one of the most difficult problems to tackle. Almost certainly there is no way in which it can be eliminated. There are almost limitless outlets for the determined person or group and unfortunately the very nature of the act provides the perpetrator with precisely what he seeks: publicity. A terrorist uses an airliner purely to draw attention to his cause and the aviation industry itself is not his prime target; it happens to be about the easiest and most effective way to achieve success. Certainly there have been many instances of lax security at airports both at home and abroad, but while there is ample scope for improvement, it is humanly impossible for every possible line of entry to be sealed.

Although this is a growing problem, it is not new. In 1950, on board a Viking of British European Airways, a bomb exploded in the galley and seriously injured the stewardess, but as the aircraft at that time were not pressurised there was no secondary effect and the aircraft landed safely. No reason for this isolated incident was discovered and no-one claimed to have placed the device on the aeroplane. In 67

An abused gift

The only good thing to come out of an aircraft accident is experience which, hopefully, will prevent a similar or identical accident from happening again. The principal distiller of that experience is the inspectorate which investigates the accident. The vital links in passing that experience on to those on the ground and in the air are the formal opinions and reports of that inspectorate, and the recommendations and directives which arise from them.

The system is, in general, efficient, honest, and unbiased wherever in the world the incident may have occurred. Even traditionally secretive countries increasingly see the need to report on accidents and their causes in the interest of improved international safety.

Increasingly, this information is not saved up until the inspectorate has finished its deliberations, months or even years after the event, but is made public as quickly as possible, as each stage in the investigation is passed. Serious problems, or potential problems, have always been passed to operators as they became known or suspected, but this industry should not have the privilege, where other industries do not, of being its own monitor. The people have a right to know, and lawmakers, rulemakers, and politicians have a right to be appraised of the various details as they become clear.

Recent events, such as the crash of the British Midland Boeing 737, have raised very real fears, however, that such information is in danger of being hijacked or discredited by a combination of vested interest, over-hasty judgement, and a lamentable desire of the popular press to find instant scapegoats. The end result might be that the trend to more open interim reporting is reversed, and that inspectorates may revert to holding on to their findings until they are complete, and can be presented in a watertight and unequivocal manner.

The British Midland case is a classic example of what can go wrong. At each stage, as investigators have released their interim findings, the popular press, "experts", and vested interests on both sides of the Atlantic have leaped to new conclusions.

Those conclusions have mostly been contradictory from one day to the next. Those conclusions have in many cases been unequivocal and absolute, ignoring the careful qualifications which the investigators have, quite rightly, included in every one of their statements. Those conclusions have jumped from unrealistic commendation to unjust condemnation. Far worse, many of these instant judgements have come from people or organisations from whom the industry and the public have every right to expect far better.

Such judgements apparently satisfy the demands of today's newspaper reader or television watcher for a black-and-white conclusion. They may also soothe the bruised egos of those whose actions may have been called into question, and they may satisfactorily transfer—albeit only briefly—the spotlight of attention on to some other suspect.

What they do not do is advance the cause of safety, or of public confidence in the industry, or of greater knowledge. In short, they act against the aims of the investigators who have made so many strides in speeding the flow of information to those who need it.

There is no doubt that the aviation industry, its regulators, and customers need a rapid flow of information after an accident, and need accurate interpretation of that information, in order to take precautions which may prevent another occurrence. There is no doubt that some of that interpretation must come into the category of "best guess" rather than absolute certainty. It therefore becomes the absolute responsibility of all those charged with passing on that information and interpretation to do so with care.

Speedily available, readily available post-crash information is a precious and fragile gift from which this industry can derive great benefit. If it is lost or damaged because of the selfish actions of an irresponsible few, the only good to come from a crash will disappear.

The leader in Flight International *for 21st January 1989 takes to task those representatives of the Press who do so much harm to serious accident investigation by supplying 'instant answers' to complex issues.*

fact, this business of announcing a claim for success is the angle that needs the closest attention, for in the unlikely event that *all* sections of the media would agree not to release such publicity-seeking information, the terrorists' cause would flounder and soon fall flat. It might be impossible to achieve, but possibly it is the only fully effective way of eliminating the trouble; if it cannot be carried out voluntarily, surely it is worth the Government's while to see if it can be enforced?

There are numerous stories about people entering airports and walking about 'airside' without challenge. In a broadcast on BBC Radio 4 on 3rd January 1989, one speaker claimed to have parked his car in a staff car park at Gatwick, walked into a hangar, stood among and touched aircraft being serviced and remained for a while leaning on a fuel bowser. He was wearing ordinary clothes and, he stated, anyone who wished to do so could see that he was not a staff member. Eventually he walked away and returned to his car unchallenged. A few days later two different but broadly comparable experiences were revealed in relation to Heathrow, when two journalists posed as cleaners and gained unsupervised access to air transport aircraft. Our national tendency is to be heavily critical of the management of any airport at which an incursion can work successfully, but airports were not designed or built as military bases and it would not be practicable (even if possible) for all places to be on top alert for every hour of every day. However, perhaps there is scope for better lines of communication between government intelligence agencies, police and the airports, so that security precautions can be stiffened when an alert is received.

Following the two Heathrow entries, the subject of security attracted the attention of politicians and in the Commons on 16th January 1989 Paul Channon said that 'British airports have a reputation internationally of very good security', to which John Prescott, Labour's transport spokesman replied 'after your performance this afternoon, people will not be assured you are any more on top of the job on this occasion than you were before'. After this customary inter-party bickering the talk in the House on this occasion extended to staff, where there has tended to be an automatic assumption that anyone who works at an airport – especially if wearing a uniform – must be wholly above board in all respects. Now, however, plans are being introduced that call for a person to serve in an airport post for six months before being granted a pass that allows unescorted access to restricted areas.

Also, David Marshall, Chairman of the House of Commons Transport Committee announced:

Three years ago the Committee conducted an inquiry into and published a report on airport security. We made 21 recommendations, the majority of which were accepted by the Government. The Committee has decided to conduct a follow-up inquiry into airport security, to examine how its recommendations have been implemented and their implementation monitored, and whether those recommendations which the Government did not accept are all the more valid today. The Committee will also look at the question of who should pay for improved security and whether the police should have an overall responsibilty for airport security matters.

All evidence was taken in private but after the inquiry a full report will be published. The Committee's terms of references were:

1. To establish the current position regarding security at airports within the UK with particular reference to:
   a) the organisation, co-ordination and financing of airport security measures
   b) control of access, perimeter fences and restricted areas
   c) checking of passengers, ground and air staff and especially checking of:
      i) boarding passengers and their hand luggage
      ii) luggage and freight to be carried in the hold of passenger-carrying aircraft
2. To ascertain what additional security methods, technical innovations and new equipment are available.

The extent to which baggage is checked is an especially important matter. I could write pages on this alone, but I will mention just two tales that I have been told. One passenger travelled from Amsterdam, where his luggage *was* checked, to the United States via Heathrow, where he changed aircraft, but where no-one showed any interest in his luggage; so the situation in this respect was 'safe' for the short first leg, but 'open' for the long haul across the Atlantic. Another traveller regularly carried a hand-gun (legally) across the Atlantic and was regularly strip-checked in the USA, but not checked at any time at Heathrow. The same passenger claims to have made several flights from Gatwick (with the gun) but always passed through unchecked.

Very frequently bags of mail are loaded aboard without investigation, and even at places where checks are made, people who arrive late for their flights are rushed through in order not to delay the scheduled departure. Flightcrew baggage, of course, is another problem to be tackled, for even if all employees are loyal, there is the possibility that their luggage, which usually is unchecked, can be used without the owner's knowledge.

Clearly security is at the top of the priority pile in current attempts to improve safety. Following the Lockerbie accident, the Secretary of State for Transport made repeated statements throughout January and February 1989 and clearly the present proposals for tightening the system will not be the last that we will hear. Sir Norman Payne, Chairman of BAA, produced a report identifying more that 100 points that can, will or should be acted upon at their own airports, and progressively these are being – and many have been – introduced. The problem, though, cannot be eliminated. By their size and the essential nature of their activities, involving large numbers of people who must be able to reach their various places of work in a very wide range of duties, airports are impossible places to protect in all ways at all times. What is worrying, though, is the need for a disaster to occur before the many easily-curable weaknesses are detected.

There are numerous other ways in which an aeroplane and its occupants can be in a critical situation, but, in the main, most of these are not terminally dangerous. In normal circumstances an engine failure on a modern airliner is not unduly hazardous, even though some elements within the media may use such an occurrence to splash across the front pages. When a Boeing 747 suffered a power loss on take-off from Gatwick, *Today* reported the incident thus on 31st March 1988 under the heading 'HOLIDAY COUPLE SUE OVER TERROR ON JET': 'A couple who were convinced that they were going to die when their holiday jumbo came within feet of disaster are suing the airline for negligence. David and Sally Woodbury were among 425 people on the jet which narrowly missed a farmhouse when an engine failed on take-off. They claim the crew were disorganised and panic-stricken as the plane skimmed tree tops and struggled to gain height'. Quite how a passenger with no aviation experience can assess a situation to declare that he is convinced that he is going to die, and how a paper can consider such an assessment to have any news value is difficult to grasp; but if there was any news beyond the relative rarity of a power failure on take-off, it should have been that the aircraft climbed to 4000 feet, dumped some fuel to bring the weight down to the permitted figure for a landing and then returned to Gatwick safely. From a public information angle, the rest is irrelevant.

Sometimes secondary problems create more difficulty than the primary failure. Although I refuse to be guilty of attempting to prejudge the cause of the East Midlands accident in January 1989, without doubt this has brought to light the fact that wiring problems on certain Boeing types could be causes for trouble. I have evidence that questions about quality control at the Boeing plant were being asked more than two years before this, but few people other than those closely involved were very interested. *After* an accident, suddenly such a subject becomes everyone's concern. By February 1989, after pressure from Europe and Japan, strong directives were issued by the US Federal Aviation Administration calling for specific safety checks on all aircraft built by Boeing since 31st December 1980, totalling 1,755 machines. The defects relate mainly to wiring and plumbing of fire detection and extinguisher systems; the instruction affected 124 aircraft operated by British airlines. Whilst to know the reason for this apparent weakness in production standards at such a vast manufacturing centre is no comfort, in practice it is a reflection of the company's success on the sales front. Unexpectedly large orders led to delivery dates that were unacceptable to the airline customers and the build-rate was increased substantially. This called for a recruiting campaign for more workers, many of whom lacked the necessary experience and skill . . . need I say more? One can round-off the argument by criticising both the internal inspection procedures and the airworthiness authority, but clearly for some time there has been a need for action; now, belatedly, it is happening.

On my desk as I write this I have a small pile of reports of defects discovered on Boeing aircraft; this should be seen not just in condemnatory terms, but as evidence that these faults have been discovered and action has been taken. The increasing age of aircraft adds further complications and many failures come to light only after a type has seen long service. I must stress, however, that while the operating industry is notified of such problems and checks are made on their own fleets, by far the greater number of failings are relatively minor in overall safety terms.

Because many airliners remain in service for longer than their designed lives, in March 1989 the CAA issued a news release explaining that twelve years previously they had instituted Structural Integrity Audits (SIAs). These cover inspections of all vulnerable parts, with a continuing replacement programme intended to ensure that neither fatigue nor corrosion will hazard safe operation. The paper quotes that there are 421 UK-registered public transport jet aircraft (even fewer than I found during an earlier check) and only 38 of these are more than 20 years old.

Occasionally items come adrift. When in May 1988 a metal door weighing 70 lb from a Boeing 727 fell into a garden at Pinner, an engineering spokesman from Heathrow was reported in *The Independent* as saying 'Bits fall off aircraft most often when they are landing or taking-off when the airframe is most stressed.' Fortunately all aircraft are designed and built to practices and standards that allow various component parts to malfunction without making machines unsafe to fly. There are laid-down procedures for pilots, who are allowed to accept minor items of unserviceability (but not missing doors!) on condition that they are logged and receive attention when practicable. Not only is this safe; it is essential if schedules are to be maintained.

Another point involving engines is a long-standing question about how many we should have. In days when airliners had piston engines, the failure rate was substantially greater than it is with modern power plants, so all long-range services were flown with four-engine types. This practice continued into the jet era and any aircraft with only two engines was restricted in the distance that it could fly – measured in time terms – from a suitably equipped airport. This is laid down by agreement through the International Civil Aviation Organisation (ICAO) and, until recently, the requirement for an aeroplane carrying 200 or more people was that its route must be within 90 minutes of an acceptable diversion. This was increased to 120 minutes and now the proposal is for a time extension to 180 minutes. The thought of flying for three hours on one engine over the Atlantic or any other ocean holds little appeal to some people and I confess to being in the front of that cowards' queue, but we must hope that any decision will be based solely on accurate statistical evidence and not influenced by commercial pressures.

If we are concerned about the aeroplanes, their engines and the related equipment, we must not forget the people who do the flying. If aircraft can deteriorate through tiredness, what about pilots? As long ago as November 1987 the CAA issued a positively-worded warning that the laid-down hours must not be exceeded and that the Authority's Flight Operations Inspectors had been instructed to be particularly vigilant in investigating this aspect on their routine checks. Airlines were to ensure that their schedules were realistic, that their rostering practices took account of sleep patterns and meal times and that transitions between day and night duties were both sensibly planned and properly observed. In both December 1988 and January 1989 stronger warnings were issued, telling operators that many may need to improve their rostering arrangements for the 1989 peak season. A new edition of CAP 371 (The Avoidance of Excessive Fatigue in Aircrew) contains revised and more stringent rules that will come into force in April 1990.

Although for several years this has been seen as a subject needing constant monitoring, the summer of 1988 brought several instances to the surface. One pilot is known to have written to the CAA demanding that the Authority takes action 'since the airlines are not capable of regulating themselves'. This expressed the feeling of many others. Perhaps the most publicised of the results of fatigue was the case of the captain who aligned his fully-loaded aircraft for a landing on the M56 motorway instead of the nearby Manchester airport. Eventually the co-pilot noticed the error and the landing was aborted at a very late stage. A report in *The Independent* on 20th August 1988 quoted a co-pilot whose captain invited him to take occasional cat-naps on long hauls, but who tried not to do so because he feared that the captain, too, might nod off. The problem on long sectors is that there is relatively little to do to occupy a crew's attention during the cruise stage, but both pilots must be alert for the eventual let-down and landing, the more so if the destination weather is marginal. Not surprisingly, allegations by crews about working excessive hours are rebuffed by the operators, one of whom retorted: 'If pilots are fatigued it's due to how they govern their lives and look after themselves, not the hours we roster.' Unfortunately the growing pilot shortage will increase the pressures on both sides.

Although generally the results of excessive fatigue are for pilots to forget to carry out their routine checks and/or to make mistakes of judgement, the problem extends into other aspects of airspace safety and might be a contributory factor in the high percentage of reports of airmisses that arc attributed to late sightings by one or both participants. Also, pilot workload in and around terminal areas, especially with single-pilot operations that are the norm in general aviation, must claim a place in the probability pattern.

Fire, of course, is a potential hazard anywhere and is not restricted to aircraft or even to other forms of transport. Quite apart from the problems that have been identified on the Boeing fleet, research into the subject continues incessantly, and in December 1988 the CAA announced plans to conduct development trials of water spray systems designed to prevent the spread of fire and therefore increase the likelihood of survivability. Tests are being conducted on wide-bodied and narrow-bodied aircraft types, but have started with trials using an old Boeing 707 fuselage at Cardington in Bedfordshire. Various alternative systems, including one combining compressed air with water are to be included in the trial. These experiments, with others to test methods of escape from burning aircraft, including improvements to colour marking schemes for quick identification of crash exits, stem largely from the accident on the ground at Manchester Airport in 1985, when 55 people died despite the emergency services being on the scene.

Then we come back to the old argument about seats: whether they should be forward or aft facing. In a letter from Ronald Ashford, the Director of the Safety Regulation Group of the CAA published in *The Times* on 19th January 1989, several interesting points emerged. In brief, he agreed that by facing aft in an accident involving large forward decelerations, there would be less likelihood of spinal injury, but with sideways acceleration and objects falling forwards from the overhead lockers a forward facing seat would offer better protection. He admits that for many years the Authority has favoured aft-facing seats, but that they have not been accepted by the travelling public. New seat-strength standards are being proposed, as are improvements to energy-absorbing characteristics, but until more information is available the Authority retains an open mind. Whatever the outcome, again we must ensure and insist on the decision being based wholly on safety evidence and not on those ever-recurring commercial pressures which so often pull clouds across the clarity of vision.

I could continue this chapter for many more pages, but as many of the points under this heading are only marginally related to *airspace* safety, perhaps the next few paragraphs will suffice before we move our minds on to another topic. Ever-tightening cash constraints in some quarters are seen as possible sources of lowered safety standards and the case that comes immediately to the fore is the reduced level of meteorological information now available. For many years pilots obtained face-to-face briefings with forecasters or spoke to them over the telephone. Forecasters were based throughout the UK and often an individual's local knowledge of his own area was very helpful. Now, however, in the interests of economy, all such services have been withdrawn and most of us (especially in general aviation) need to rely mainly on a recorded Airmet facility. This is not the place for detail, but many of us have suffered problems with this reduced level of information and, as the result of inputs from users, the service has been slightly improved. However, it is a poor substitute for the personal touch. One experienced flying instructor's experience is expressed in these three paragraphs from a letter by Rufus Heald published in *Flight International* dated 21st January

1989 under the heading 'An unwelcome weather change':

> During 1988 I noticed that general-aviation accident statistics have showed an unfortunate upward trend. The reports indicate that in many cases weather has been a contributory factor, before or during the event. Maybe the pilot didn't (or couldn't) get a proper meteorological briefing before take-off, or maybe the weather deteriorated *en route* and reached a level which was beyond his skill or ability.
>
> Much has been said already about the UK's inadequate preflight briefing facilities, which do not stand comparison with the data available in more aeronautically aware countries. One of my students spent £13 on the telephone trying to obtain an adequate forecast for a route from north to south of the U.K. He failed to get the information he needed because he ran out of money.'
>
> Remember that GA aircraft comprise over 90 per cent of the aircraft on the UK register. I just hope that in a few more years we have weather control, and that the accuracy of the control exceeds the 48 per cent accuracy currently enjoyed by the forecasts.

The savings effected in the changeover are minimal by aviation standards and other people in need of weather information have been treated far less harshly: still Grannie can ring to enquire whether it will be sunny by the sea and mariners have access to detail that is denied to others who need it. In safety terms, though, perhaps this unwelcome move compares with the closure of several coastguard stations around the shores of Britain and severe reductions in the safety-centred meetings staged by the International Maritime Organisation, a London-based United Nations agency that regulates 97 per cent of the world's shipping. So flying is not the only travel mode that suffers from cut-backs in safety services on penny-pinching monetary grounds.

If this chapter gives the impression that all is far from well on the 'other risks' front, I must stress that there is an enormous amount of built-in safety in all matters relating to aircraft and aviation. Aeroplanes, engines and equipment tend to be over-engineered and operating procedures are designed to allow scope for human error and still leave margins; the results are their own best advertisements. How else could air travel retain equal first place on the safety ladder for year after year after year? This does not mean that there is scope for complacency. Research continues in all spheres of activity and the only unfortunate element in this is that usually an accident is needed to set the process moving. In short, more effort is devoted to cure than to prevention, so somewhere our priorities are misplaced.

Despite our national shortcomings, in most spheres we have better records than many other states can claim. I am indebted to the editor of *Airway,* the CAA staff journal for providing this true tale, published originally in the Authority's Occurrence Digest. Under the heading 'Who's in Charge' the text reads:

> Recently a UK aircraft descending into Dubai, under radar control from Dubai Airport, received instructions to alter course from a warship transmitting on the International Distress Frequency of 121.5 MHz. Dubai was informed and an altercation arose between the two agencies as to who was controlling the aircraft.
>
> Eventually the aircraft was turned towards the localiser for Dubai's Runway 12L and landed safely. The pilot was subsequently advised that the instructions from the warship to alter course had put the aircraft on a conflicting path with

traffic departing Sharjah.

The Authority commented on the occurrence: ICAO has been trying for some time, to obtain routes that would ensure the safe passage of international air traffic from any localised conflict in the Gulf.

Until this problem is resolved, pilots are advised to maintain a listening watch on 121.5 mHz when operating in the area. If any agency requires a flight to deviate from instructions previously given by a civil air traffic control agency, pilots should immediately make a PAN call confirming their actions to all the ATC agencies in the area.

In the USA we find the FAA to be dissatisfied with the operating standards of many of the commuter airlines. There have been deficiencies in management personnel, who lack knowledge of complex air carrier procedures, inadequate aircraft inspection programmes, engineering directors who fail to understand the contents of their maintenance manuals, a chief pilot who was unaware of flight-time limitations and crew rest requirements, failures to comply with the Administration's mandatory airworthiness directives and companies flying aircraft for long periods after known defects have been reported but not rectified. Long before you read this, though, the FAA inspectorate will have visited all 173 commuter airlines to check what progress has been achieved.

Finally, in our choice of selected examples of inadequacies in other parts of the world, I am indebted to *Flight International* for information about air traffic control in the Soviet Union. The journal *Grazhdanskaya Aviatsiya* states that the standard of control across the country is far from consistent and there is reference to dangers of collision during take-off and landing and the need to abort take-offs due to actions by air traffic controllers. There is reference to poor management, the need for more effectively balanced working teams and for duties to be better allocated. Until recently the first-attempt success rate among trainees taking their qualifying tests and examinations was only just over 15 per cent. The journal stresses the importance of the English language in the syllabus because a significant proportion of airmisses (I wonder how many they have) occur between Aeroflot aircraft and those of foreign operators.

I mention these not to point fingers of condemnation at others in an attempt to hide the deficiencies at home, but to make clear that, whatever our weaknesses on the safety front, we are far from alone in our problems. Much work remains ahead if we are to improve our standards in all the spheres mentioned in this chapter, but, with one unfortunate exception, solutions should be found to the problems that have been faced. The odd card in the pack, though, is the level of security needed to prevent terrorism, as the extent of the success achieved will be quantifiable only in negative terms. A year without an aeroplane being hijacked or blown up in flight will not prove that all the measures have worked; only an accident as a result of terrorist activity will prove that they have failed. So we must hope that the question will remain unanswered for so long that, eventually, we will feel sufficiently confident to suggest that one of today's worst enemies exists only in the history books.

Chapter 9
The Case
for the Defence

NO-ONE SHOULD wish to commit a country to war and every sensible move should be made to avoid it, but a nation filled with conscientious-objectors would find its freedom constrained on a very short-term lease. Almost every state in the world recognises the need to defend its territory and even those that have managed to retain neutrality in all recent conflicts – such as Switzerland – have armed forces that are appropriate to their sizes and to their geographical situations. In fact the Swiss are very conscious of the importance of national security, not only with regular full-time units, but with well-trained and well-equipped part-time reserve strengths. Many of their front-line military aircraft are flown by these reservists.

I mention this because in the past Britain operated on a comparable basis. RAF reserve flying schools and squadrons of the Royal Auxiliary Air Force were to be found all over our island and these needed freedom of airspace to operate alongside the regular units. Then, though, we had not developed the habit of complaining about every activity in which we ourselves do not participate. The air over Britain was filled with far more aeroplanes than it is today and there were very few cases of the various sectors of aviation moaning miserably about each others' intrusions into someone else's patch. Civil and military, fast and slow (yes, some were quite fast), large and small 'mixed it' quite happily and I am far from alone in remembering the hand-wave recognitions that we gave to each other when meeting other aeroplanes. Clearly I recall the day when I saw a Dutch Air Force Meteor alongside me, at a sensibly safe distance, but close enough to recognise hand gestures. I gave him a salute, he tucked in and formated for several minutes, removing his oxygen mask so that I could see his smile before he gave a thumbs-up and broke away. I have no idea who he was, or where he was from, or why, but clearly we both enjoyed the friendly encounter and such a practice was not uncommon. Think about it a bit and you will find that it could be beneficial.

I tell another, slightly earlier, tale, not to 'shoot a line' but to lay stress on a point that is significant to the cause of this chapter. I was engaged mainly on high-altitude work, but with occasional forays into low-level sorties. Not only did the latter provide us with essential training, but because of their relative rarity they were particularly enjoyable. On one occasion, alas, I overstepped my brief very slightly and, at the tender age of 21, I was 'invited' to explain my actions before the famous Wing Commander (later Air Commodore) Hughie Idwal Edwards, VC, whose short suffix was his deserving award for his noted exploits in the Second World War. From a safe distance I had viewed him as a fierce man and as I was kept waiting for a seemingly inordinate time, possibly as a planned part of the punishment, I suffered all the pains that an imaginative mind can create. Would I be grounded? Was my flying career finished?

Eventually I was directed coldly into the boss's sanctum. 'So you've been low flying.' 'Yes, Sir.' Long pause. 'Why?' Quick think. 'Because I feel that we need more of it to maintain our standards – Sir.' Longer pause. 'You don't think that at all. You enjoyed it, didn't you?' Of course I had or I wouldn't have done it, so, 'Yes, Sir'. The longest pause of all. Much fear. 'We must do something about people like you. Other people don't like it – you should know that – you should take more care where you go. Of course you'll do it again, but make sure you don't need to come before me when you get caught.' Silence. What do I do now? In best fourth-form style I mustered 'Is that all, Sir?' 'Do you want any more? Go.'

The next morning, to my surprise and pleasure, I found that I had been authorised to carry out a long navigational exercise, *all* at low level. At the time my only thought was that the Wing Commander was a remarkably considerate chap, but much later I realised that this was the most sensible decision that anyone could have made. At that age, though, human psychology was not one of my top-ranking subjects.

All flying – and especially military flying – needs to be disciplined, but in itself this does not mean that it must be oppressively restrained. Aviation in the Services calls for an attitude and outlook that is far distanced from the needs of the airline pilot or the private flier. A member of a first-line squadron who has no 'spirit' in peaceful surroundings is less likely to put his energies into a wartime task than is a colleague who becomes an integral part of the machine to which he is attached. If his aeroplane has potential, so must he be in harmony with the scope that such potential creates. He must be able to operate, and be experienced in operating, his mount and related equipment to their permitted limits. Otherwise, if caught in anger, he – and on a larger scale his nation – will prove to be the loser.

In earlier years much operational flying took place at high level. There was a phase in the late fifties and into the sixties when, because of this, Service aeroplanes were relatively rare sights and sounds. In broad terms unless you were in the immediate vicinity of a military airfield, you could be unaware that much activity was taking place. In fact, some people remarked that if the Services failed to participate in flying displays, many would be virtually unaware of their existence. This might have suited those who object to aeroplanes flying at low level in the vicinities of their homes and workplaces, but unless there is some unpredictable change in tactics we must learn to live with the changed circumstances of today.

Much operational flying must take place at low level. Primarily this is for purposes of survival, to enable the enemy to be given shock treatment from aircraft that have penetrated the defended area without being traced on radar. Unfortunately, with improved equipment on the ground, detection has become possible at progressively reduced heights and to counter this, the attacking machines have needed to fly steadily lower. With a modern high-speed fighting aeroplane, the lower the level, the more difficult the task, so the greater is the need both for formal training and constant continuation flying. These procedures

78   *A BAe Hawk during a typical low-level sortie in the UK.*

must be practised over territory that simulates the surroundings in which real action is likely to occur, so a variety of areas must be available; this is why parts of Scotland, Wales and Cumbria must be used. Each year about 150,000 low-level training missions must be flown over the UK by the British and allied forces within NATO, so someone must find the necessary space to enable these to operate safely.

At one time Britain hosted a number of set, clearly-defined low-flying routes and all aircraft that needed to operate below normal heights were allocated slots in these grooves. For various reasons, however, not the least of which was a persistent string of complaints from people who lived under them, the pattern was changed and exercises at the lower levels were extended to a far greater proportion of the UK. Although this reduced the frequency of the moans from the original sources, predictably the pattern of the objections expanded to match the increased area of coverage. More recently, in December 1988, the plan was modified again to allot separate times for RAF Strike Command, RAF Germany and the US Air Force and, for night flying, to introduce a broadly clockwise pattern around the system. This was introduced to minimise the risk of collision. Even before this, however, pilots were required to book their flights centrally through a special tactical cell at RAF West Drayton in Middlesex. Also, for many years, a Civil Aircraft Notification Procedure (CANP) has enabled civil pilots on essential low level tasks, such as crop spraying and pipeline work, to liaise with the Services so that there can be mutual knowledge of each other's intended presence. So, despite frequent shouts to the contrary, it is not and has not been wholly haphazard.

Clearly there are a few people who have genuine and even plausible causes to complain, but in many cases selfishness is the prime mover. 'Take it from me and give it to someone over there' might be the theme, just as it is with plans for the construction of new motorways. Still the parish pump rules. The salient point, though, is that if Britain is to fulfil its obligations to NATO *and* maintain its own defence capability to ensure the continued freedom that we enjoy, the Services *must* carry out an extensive programme of aircrew training at low levels.

Unfortunately the complaints originating from private residents – some of which may be excusable because the people concerned are unaware of the need – are not the only ones with which the Ministry of Defence needs to contend. Complaints from other airspace users (especially where commercial interests are affected), from controllers and from civil aerodrome operators are not uncommon. In one case an airport manager lodged an objection because a pair of RAF Hawks flew in the vicinity when an airliner was on the approach to land. As is the custom, the airliner was lined-up many miles from touchdown and was well clear of regulated airspace, so why, oh why, does the machine operating purely for commercial gain justify any priority over a couple of aircraft that were airborne with equal justification and possibly for a more nationally-significant purpose? If an airline pilot or a controller geared to similar thinking finds another aeroplane using the sky that belongs to Britain, automatically there is an assumption that the other machine is the one in the way. Politicians and the press, too, fall for this erroneous assessment, but fortunately if an airmiss is reported, the matter is handled subsequently by the encouragingly impartial Joint Airmiss Working Group.

The tendency to jump to a mentally preset conclusion is comparable with the media reports about accidents at level crossings. Almost always a train is reported as hitting a car or a lorry, therefore by implication casting blame on the train driver, but the rules are very clear and the person in charge of the road vehicle (unless it has failed at an unfortunate moment) has no right nor cause to be there. Although the train *did* hit the vehicle, usually the fault lay with the driver of the latter for undisciplined behaviour. A more reasonable presentation in the press would be that a car driver who stopped on the crossing, or who tried to rush over it when he should have stopped, caused a train to have an accident. So let us hear, at least occasionally, that the presence of a commercial aircraft causes concern to the pilot of a Service aeroplane or a light civil machine.

In Chapter 7 I mention that the affairs of Parliament would be treated with greater respect if Members could learn to restrict their topics for judgement to those that they understand. Certainly freedom of speech is an essential part of democracy, but cautious choice of subject can be equally valuable and any MP who speaks in a way that undermines the nation's defence responsibilities cannot be doing justice to anyone's interests. The matter concerned may be one of local interest to the constituents who elected him, but when this leads to the bold headline 'Local MP wants ban on low flying by RAF jets' (*The Independent,* 29th December 1988) this can create waves of difficulty for many people. In short, many of the criticisms of the press that I make in Chapter 7 are sparked by incautious comments in the House; in this case, the paper was reporting correctly the unwise statement that had been made.

Let me quote another example. After the unfortunate incident on 9th August 1988 in which two Tornados collided over Cumbria, opposition MPs started the usual clamour for restrictions on low flying by military aircraft, headed by Dale Campbell-Savors (Labour, Workington) who stated 'The whole programme is completely out of control.' Fortunately, however, the Member for the area concerned responded with a more meaningful reaction to the situation. In the past ten years, we learn, 624 people had been killed on the roads of Cumbria and 120 had died in the mountains, but not one civilian had been killed as a result of a military flying accident over the county. The chances of two operational military aeroplanes on totally unrelated missions making physical contact in such a situation are unbelievably remote (the new one-way system should make the likelihood even less so), but to make a parochial call for a ban in one area – bearing in mind that the work *must* be carried out somewhere – merely places more stress on airspace elsewhere and increases the risk of accident.

Perhaps it is relevant here to state that the flying carried out by the Services covers the widest range of activity of all sectors. From small single-engine Chipmunks and Bulldogs (which come in the light aeroplane category), through many shapes and sizes of helicopters; Jet Provosts and Hawks; front-line Tornados, Harriers, Jaguars and Phantoms; Dominies and BAe 125s which are equivalent to the business jets of the civil world; Andovers (which are virtually militarised BAe 748 airliners), Hercules and VC-10s in the heavier transport role; and BAe 146s of the Queen's Flight. Then there are even self-launching motor gliders used for cadet training. So the Royal Air Force alone covers the entire spectrum of flying and in many cases its crews need to operate in far more demanding conditions and situations than ever apply to those in any of the civil sectors. Numbers may be fewer than in the past, but, allowing for attrition, the RAF's Tornado order alone amounts to no fewer than 435 aircraft. Remember that our *total* civil air transport fleet of all types comprises only 685 aircraft, so when considering overall requirements the airspace planners have duties to look more deeply at the needs of *all* users. Although I have given specific mention to the RAF, we must not overlook the operational and training commitments that must be fulfilled by aeroplanes and helicopters of the Royal Navy and the British Army.

For several years I have been surprised at the relatively ineffective – almost timid – manner in which the airspace and other requirements for military flying have been handled. The leaves of history show clearly enough what happens to a nation that fails to maintain adequate defences and this background alone should provide sufficient evidence to give moral strength to those whose task it is to fight for our ability to fight. Members of Parliament flying their parochial flags in attempts to restrain the essential activities of the flying Services – and because it is the largest, the RAF receives nearly all the verbal or journalistic flak – are met with promises of attempts to find ways to alleviate whatever the alleged problems may be. Yet those whose task it is to defend the defence should be able to see themselves batting on sound wickets and turn the attack onto the critics. Service flying is essential if we are to secure our future and, without adequate training areas to enable it to remain effective, one day we could find ourselves unable to enjoy those holiday flights that seem so important in our short-term thinking. Or is there a deeper problem because military flying – as opposed to a military contract – fails to have the commercial pull that some of the other aviation activities attract?

When Britain was fighting to retain freedom and a way of life that goes with it, the civilian public was overjoyed to see Hurricanes, Spitfires, Lancasters and others all over the skies. When they flew past at low level, many people stopped and waved to show that their presence was welcome. Some of those who complain today cannot have experienced the reality of the need for an effective defence system, but most probably many others are of an older generation that is suffering from a convenient loss of memory. If ever we should be in the unhappy position of being forced into war again – and a strong defence is the surest way of avoiding that likelihood – I hope that those who whinge now will recall their past weakness; or, if they fail to do so, perhaps others will remember it.

Chapter 10
Who are
these Fun Fliers?

FOR SEVERAL YEARS we have heard derogatory remarks aimed at those people who have no need to take to the air and clutter our airspace: the fun fliers. So I have endeavoured to discover who these people are and whether they are really the high level of problem that so many critics accuse them of being. In the process I unearthed some revealing information and surprised myself by discovering that by far the majority of general aviation activity is serious business in one form or another. So I faced a difficulty: Who are these people who fly for fun?

Then, quite unexpectedly, the truth appeared on my desk. In a speech to the Tour Operators Study Group, Christopher Tugendhat, Chairman of the CAA, had announced that of all passenger-carrying flights from UK airports outside the London area, an astonishing 87 per cent of the occupied seats were filled with holidaymakers on cheap charter flights. Even when London's airports are brought into the calculations, 55 per cent of all filled seats fall into this category. He warned operators that most probably there was too much holiday capacity on offer, that margins were tightly squeezed and that these were problems for the industry to tackle. Another warning point from Mr Tugendhat was that 'many holidays were sold at prices that could simply not be sustained.' This speech was made in June 1987.

Almost exactly a year later some more truths emerged. Despite an increase in turnover of 31 per cent in a year's trading, the operators had managed a net loss of nearly £25 million. In fact, between them, eleven companies managed to lose £48.3 million and the £23.5 million profit by the remaining 19 organisations were needed to contain the trade's overall deficit within the quarter-century. Not surprisingly, by July 1988 the Air Travel Trust Committee published in its annual report that 16 companies had failed in the year, that 8000 passengers had been flown home at the expense of bonds and 18,000 booked customers had been let down by firms that had collapsed.

The whole truth, of course, is hard to find. When, early in 1988, the operators prepared to add fuel surcharges to their published prices, many papers took them to task. The contrasts in media handling seem to be worth quoting.

The Times on 29th March: **'Holiday Surcharge Inquiry'**

'An investigation into claims that tour operators are overcharging holidaymakers by £25 m a year has been launched by the Government'

A typical airliner dedicated to transporting holiday makers to the sun. Of the 179 people commonly carried aboard this aircraft 172 are 'fun fliers'.

The *Daily Mirror* on 30th March: **'Holiday Rip-off'**

'When we fly to the sun, the chances are we'll be ripped off rotten before reaching the airport. British holiday companies could teach an Arab bazaar a thing or two about overcharging'

Somehow it seems significant that the £25 million surcharge quoted by *The Times* equates exactly with the industry's collective loss of £25 million in the previous year.

Does this affect airspace? The answer, bluntly, is yes. If too many operators are chasing too few customers and are forced to lower their prices to the extent of producing net trading losses, more commercial air transport aircraft are flying than the true economics of the industry can stand. But that is not all. If the prices had been pitched at figures that would withstand sound commercial judgement, fewer holidaymakers would have booked the not-quite-so-cheap seats to fun in the sun and everyone, everywhere, would have been more contented. The operators would have made money for less hassle, the customers who reached their destinations would have been flown home without difficulty and there would have been no frustrated people whose holiday plans fell apart. Above all, though, as far as we are concerned here, fewer commercial air transport aircraft on the move would have caused less airspace and airport clutter and congestion during the year's peaks of activity. This is a clearcut case in which sound commercialism should have been its own traffic regulator. On 31st July 1988 the 83

Sunday Times made a case that the operators must increase their charges as they had not learned from the previous year and some were still making losses.

Despite this, the tour industry launched into the following year seeking – and obtaining – licences amounting to an increase of 15.6 per cent in the number of available holidays. Very sensibly, though, the CAA went clearly into print to point out that the level of capacity for which licences are issued is the figure for which the operators apply; it does not reflect an assessment by the Authority of the true size of the market. The *Financial Times* took a good look at business in the middle of 1988 and under the heading 'Sun, Sand and Surplus Seats' gave a well-reasoned assessment that there had been a downturn in demand of at least 5 per cent since the previous year. This did not lower the number of aircraft movements, but merely left more seats empty.

A major issue facing all airspace users is that this unrealistic growth, putting more aircraft into the air than can possibly be justified, creates problems for everyone. We hear that the airspace in the London area is congested to capacity (although we burn a few ears on this in Chapter 12), so if this is the case we need to investigate whether all the traffic should be there. If it can be accommodated into the system and provide an efficient service to the holidaymakers who seek it and pay the right money for it, the air touring facility must play a significant role in the total aviation scene, but it does not have a special right to priority treatment when it affects the operations of the other users, many of whom may need to fly for essential rather than joy-riding purposes. Also, we must remember that all these holiday flights help to increase the national deficit. As in each case British money is being spent abroad, they compare with imports and therefore result in a net financial loss to the nation. So if the operators lose money, who gains anything?

This leads to another strange activity that calls for comment. On my desk I have a sheet advertising the pleasure flights in Concorde that are taking place from Heathrow during the summer of 1989. Then someone sent me a whole page advertisement from the *Daily Mirror* announcing the British Airways 'happy hour' flights to encourage people who have not flown before to savour the delights of flying on board a modern airliner. This, presumably, is to persuade those who have not needed to travel by air that they should help to add to any congestion that may exist by creating additional demand for extra flights. Before you challenge me by saying that these joy flights take place from Manchester, let me add that any resulting additional journeys from there to the Continent would add to the problems because, almost unbelievably, they are routed via London's airspace!

Most people have sympathy in principle for the aim to increase the number of flights from the provincial airports, for almost all are grossly and sadly under-used. The constant call to move traffic departures from London to Manchester, for example, has led to whole-page advertisements appearing in leading daily newspapers, so I am not surprised to hear caustic comment when (self-styled quote) 'One of Britain's most successful holiday airlines', formed and based in Manchester, moves south to start a new series of trips from Gatwick. Business must be where business is, but if London's airports are as busy as they claim, operating, apparently, to capacity at almost all times, this seems to be counter-productive to any attempted easement of the alleged congestion and associated safety problems. On the other hand, the arrangements by one tour operator to launch continental holiday flights from Kent International (known to many as RAF Manston) makes much practical sense. It avoids the hassle of

Gatwick and starts the flights away from the most heavily congested areas – in terms of both runway and airspace availability.

A point that is plugged in too many quarters is that someone paying for his seat on a flight is entitled to total protection from all other traffic at all times, but so far no-one has offered a convincing reason why air travellers should expect some special privilege that is denied to all other transport users. If I buy a ticket for a journey on a coach or a bus, or if I hire a taxi or pay for a self-drive hire car, I have no automatic protection or separation from the juggernaut that lurches out of control across the hard shoulder and into the other carriageway; this is an experience that I have met and which, as with other motorists, I must accept as one of the hazards of needing or wishing to go from one place to another. The argument that a collision in the air must be much more serious than one on the road holds no strength, for we meet precisely the same death if we hit another car head-on at a legitimate closing speed of up to 140 mph as we do if airliners should meet at several times that figure. Also, if you contend that in many cases road accidents lead to injuries rather than certain death and that mid-air contact must be terminal, I will save you the need to turn back to Chapter 7 by reminding you about one of the very few in-flight collisions between airliners that have ever occurred in the remarkably safe history of the industry: in 1954, two passenger-carrying airliners hit each other in cloud at 11,000 feet near Paris and not one person was bodily harmed.

I have both a desire and a duty to support an improvement in the overall level of safety for users of UK airspace, but the key is the word 'overall', which must cover the entire spectrum. To seek more safety for one section of the community, even if travelling to or from fun in the sun, is a fine motive when taken in isolation from the whole scene, but when this increases congestion and reduces safety for a far larger number of aircraft and the people inside them, it reflects an unacceptably narrow view of one's responsibility to the task. I must repeat that because of personal and selfish interest in our own activities, no-one has dared to suggest that the private or business motorist should be banned from driving on most roads in order to provide special protection that will lengthen the lives of the football crowds travelling in coaches; but the situation is comparable, even to the extent of the relative numbers involved. Also, why does the sun-seeking holidaymaker justify more protection than a person on a business flight, flying his own aeroplane at his own or his company's expense to or from the continent to secure an export order? Here the argument that the charter passenger is paying for his security collapses immediately.

Safety, of course, is both subjective and emotive. Perhaps by relating this true tale I am working against one or two of the other points that I make elsewhere, but I am aiming to view the subject from the centre line. Two holiday airliners, both operated by the same company and with each captain knowing where the other was, arrived at a reporting point at the same time. They were flying in opposite directions with 2000 feet vertical separation and at this position both were due to turn onto new headings. Because one passenger was the holder of a private pilot's licence he claimed to know all about such things, so he insisted that it was an airmiss and that the pilots were taking avoiding action. He refused to accept comfort from the stewardess, insisted on lodging a formal complaint to the captain and made threats of publicising the dangers to which he had been placed through his contacts in the media. Surprisingly – and fortunately for all – the occupant of a seat two rows ahead was an air traffic control officer. With all the other passengers, he heard the fracas and only when he explained how the system 85 works and that this was a perfectly routine and planned procedure did the complainant agree to shut-up.

This story contains several messages. It confirms the dangers of knowing a little about a subject and, as a result, expressing false information to the consternation of others; that even from a position on board one aeroplane, from which the vertical separation of 2000 feet should be easy to recognise, even a person with a pilot's licence can believe that there is a dangerous situation; and that such a situation could have been the source of a false story of alarm that more than one daily tabloid would have grabbed greedily.

The main purpose of this chapter is not to denigrate the holiday air travel movement, but to place its needs and national value in perspective with the other claimants to consideration. If there is a shortage of available airspace – and from my own observations and discussions with many others there is no proven case for this – then this section of the industry must take its share and no more. Possibly with a more realistic appraisal of its failures and achievements it will find its own activity level.

Despite a request to the CAA for licences covering an increase of 4.7 per cent in the number of holidays (the smallest for several years) 1989 bookings reveal a substantial downtrend from 1988 figures and this has caused concern for many operators. In two separate surveys, both with results published early in 1989, one report confirms that in the previous year 750,000 people who bought package holidays were either 'dissatisfied' or 'totally dissatisfied' and, although this was played down by the Association of British Travel Agents (ABTA), the second survey by *Holiday Which?* claims that the general level of dissatisfaction was even worse than that discovered by the trade association.

I should point out that most of these complaints were not aimed at the flying part of the deal, but in terms of effect this is irrelevant, for if people find the hotels unsatisfactory they are unlikely to try again and the demand for holiday air travel diminshes. So perhaps, overall, the operators, which according to a meaningful report published in *The Independent* on 4th January 1989, are almost certain to see a further run of bankruptcies, will make a smaller demand on the system. Certainly the present trend makes a nonsense of the constantly rising traffic predictions that airspace planners seem to be unable to resist.

Whatever the outcome in terms of traffic figures, at least we know now who carries the handle 'the funfliers'.

Chapter 11
General Aviation

The Ministerial Directions to the CAA and NATS require the interests of all airspace users – including general aviation – to be taken into account in the planning of airspace arrangements.

THESE WORDS were written on 18th January 1989 in a letter from the Civil Aviation Policy Directorate of the Department of Transport to the Aircraft Owners and Pilots Association. They confirm the points mentioned in an earlier letter from the Department, quoted in Chapter 4, which included 'decisions on airspace are for the CAA and NATS' together with confirmation that GA requirements must be considered. Also this is stated in 'Directions to the Civil Aviation Authority' under Section 28(2) of the Civil Aviation Act.

These points are very significant to the purpose of this book. Already I have mentioned that general aviation is by far the largest sector in UK, European and world terms, but it is the section that is least understood by politicians, the public and the planners. Military aviation is the cause of many complaints in the course of its essential duties, but many people – and many who should be more fully informed – seem unaware that GA has any duties to perform. GA has needed to fight for its share of the airspace and for its rightful place at airports and some aerodromes, so the letters mentioned above form a part of some correspondence that AOPA instigated in order to have the position confirmed and clarified. Despite excuses previously offered by NATS that they sought approval for their plans from DTp, it is clear now that the responsibility rests squarely with the NATS Directorate of Control (Airspace Policy). This body is under firm Ministerial direction to ensure that GA's needs are taken into account and, with recent threats to operations in the London area, the movement has needed to combine its collective forces to reveal its strength and purpose.

So what *is* this business known as general aviation? The term originated in the USA and spread into this country when the activity known formerly as light aviation matured into a wider range of operations, thereby outgrowing its more limited title. GA today includes police, pipeline and pollution patrols, traffic surveys, ambulance flights, urgent deliveries of kidneys and other human organs needed for transplants, air survey and aerial photography, crop spraying and dusting, the civil side of search-and-rescue operations, flights for business (many of which generate export orders), pilot training, club and private flying, gliding, 87 ballooning and parachuting. It operates on a very broad base from a surprisingly large number of sites – not just licensed aerodromes – and has a very significant role in the lives of considerable numbers of citizens.

In earlier days the lighter side of aviation suffered from an unfortunate image and its participants were dubbed 'fun fliers'. Usually this term was used in a derogatory sense – sometimes based on jealousy – and was intended to portray a collection of rich and sometimes irresponsible playboys who could afford to indulge in a pastime that the masses were unable to reach. In informed quarters, however, the term has become recognised as a gross misnomer and, as I have mentioned in the previous chapter, if the expression must be retained, its usage should be transferred to an entirely different sun-seeking section of the community.

I am not saying that no-one in GA flies purely for personal pleasure. Many people do just that and long may this continue. They operate in conventional light aeroplanes, gliders, microlights and hang-gliders, under balloons and attached to parachutes. In recent times the activities have extended to parascending and paragliding and for several years in the USA there have been powered parachutes! People are determined to get themselves into the air and some of the unusual developments in the past pair of decades have been results of frustrations caused by the restrictions imposed on the use of ordinary light aircraft. So if the new breed of flier causes airspace planning problems, a few looks over shoulders might help to explain why those problems have developed. It is not too late for those in office now to think hard about how they can prevent the complications worsening over the next decade or two.

Just as marinas are appearing all over the UK to cope with the increasing number of privately-owned boats, so there is a pressing need within GA to have more airspace in which – and more bases from which – to operate. I have not heard many people complain about the larger numbers of yachts and cruisers – except perhaps on grounds of environmental erosion – yet still some people have the outdated view that GA is a luxury rather than a necessity.

Earlier in this book I mentioned that the commercial air transport sector depends, and without doubt for several years has depended, on a healthy light aviation movement for its growth and possibly its survival. After the Second World War the airline industry absorbed substantial numbers of ready-made pilots who had been trained and had obtained considerable flying experience in the Services. These people occupied most of the front seats and although steadily their numbers have been diminishing, only recently have the last of the wartime pilots reached retirement age. Certainly even today the Services continue to provide a small supply of newcomers, but the airlines could not survive on these alone and recruitment from other sources has become an established part of the pattern.

The industry has a very bad record for forecasting pilot demand and for as long as I can remember there has been either a surplus or a shortage, at times reaching acute proportions in both directions. When British Airways placed considerable numbers of trainees through the College of Air Training at Hamble in Hampshire, the eventual result was a glut of raw graduates for whom there were no posts to fill. Some of the new pilots flew as stewards and others were placed 'out to grass' on medium-term time leads. Since then the college has been closed, the supply pipe failed and another shortage arose. Today BA has placed batches through the new British Aerospace College at Prestwick, but time will reveal the success or otherwise of the airline's demand forecasting.

You may ask why all this finds its way into a chapter devoted to general aviation. The answer is that whenever there have been gaps to fill, GA has come forward as the life-line for the survival of the commercial air transport sector. The important point, though, is that this is not through preplanned, organised, subsidised or sponsored training schemes, but wholly through the initiative of – and almost entirely at the expense of – the people who wish to qualify to fly professionally. What is more important is that many of these are unaware of their intentions or ambitions until they have joined their local flying clubs, obtained their private pilots' licences and then have been bitten by the idea of earning their livings from flying. So it is incorrect to say that only a few of the people flying in the private sector are doing so on their ways to aviation careers, for large numbers of people need to train as private pilots for the required figures to emerge at the airline entry stage. This is not because they are incapable of reaching the necessary standards, but due to the many difficulties that arise as *en route* obstacles. Not the least of those is the cost; and to achieve their aims, many aspiring pilots give up most of life's luxuries and live very frugally.

There are various paths along what is known as the 'self-improver' route, but whichever method is used the expense to the individual is very substantial. There is no way of avoiding the costs of the earlier stages, but along the line it is possible to qualify for the new Basic Commercial Pilot's Licence (BCPL) and take a course for the Assistant Flying Instructor's (AFI) Rating. Once a candidate has obtained the required experience and these qualifications, he can gain employment as an assistant instructor. Rightly he is required to operate under the supervision of a more experienced person who holds a full Instructor's Rating, but he is able to teach newcomers to the art of flying and in the process he obtains valuable experience towards his ultimate goal. In this way the training system gains a constant supply of new junior instructors, but unfortunately most of these are attracted by the appeal of the gold (in more than one sense) offered by the airlines, so few – far too few – stay in GA to make careers in this sector. The arrangement works, however, and in the past year no fewer than 320 pilots entered the profession via this means. Also, we must not overlook the fact that these people presented themselves at virtually no cost to their prospective employers, so through their personal pockets they provided heavy subsidies for the operators, who otherwise would have needed to dig deeply into their corporate earnings to sponsor *ab initio* training schemes. Now, belatedly, a few companies have taken this step, but only because they see it as the only way to keep their aircraft flying and the revenue coming in. To train 10 pilots for their Commercial Licences and Instrument Ratings from 'scratch' today would cost £½ m, so the airlines should be very grateful for the 'free gifts' that GA has provided. How many airliners would be grounded already if the ready-made supply had not been available through the efforts and enthusiasm of the self-financed people within the GA movement?

Few people appear to appreciate the significance of general aviation as an essential component in the overall operating pattern. The constant flow of new pilots to the profession must not only continue, but if the forecast airline traffic figures have any meaning (challenged in Chapter 14) then very large increases in numbers of newcomers will be required. If the club and private side of flying is not given more freedom of scope and space, enabling people to learn to fly and qualify to higher levels largely at their own expense, then the commercial air transport industry will need to plan drastic reductions in the scale of its operations. The potential here is not missed by a few people with eyes to 89 prospective business, for I have received a letter from Australia's Senior Trade Commissioner in London, suggesting that candidates may find advantages in carrying out their training there rather than in the UK. Anyone concerned with the British national economy should reflect on that. Already one UK airline has obtained its recent pilot recruits from Australia.

In addition to its importance as a pipeline in pilot supply, general aviation has a lead role in world and national economics and a few figures from the EC Air Transport Policy Document (Civil Aviation Memorandum No 2) may bring the picture into perspective. Paragraph 4.4.2.4. states that GA accounts for 96 per cent of the total number of civil aircraft in the western world, 96 per cent of pilots, 80 per cent of all civil aviation flying hours and more than 50 per cent of the world's air passenger traffic. Yet its 300,000 aircraft consume less than 7 per cent of the fuel used by civil aviation. The document continues 'General aviation makes an effective contribution to the economic activity of individual countries by providing them with a flexible means of transport (even in regions away from main traffic flows) and by supporting a relatively high-tech industry employing a skilled labour force. General aviation constitutes the biggest and most rapidly expanding market . . . .'

Paragraph 4.4.2.5. states 'It ought to be possible to remove some of the main obstacles to the development of general aviation in Europe. The European Community could play a decisive role in this respect by taking measures designed to guarantee the promotion of general aviation within the frame work of regional development policy . . . .' As a significant comparison with the figure of 300,000 GA aircraft, the International Air Transport Association has announced a world airliner fleet strength of 5,600 aircraft. Certainly some airlines are not in IATA membership, but it includes the major carriers; and, predictably, all the world's largest fleets are American, with six operators each having substantially more than 200 aircraft on their books.

The EC document does not refer just to the UK, for aviation is essentially an international activity and what happens in Europe and in other parts of the western world must apply in Britain. Unless as a nation we are to stagnate in aviation terms, we have a duty to take GA seriously and to encourage its promotion. This will necessitate some practical rethinking by many people, including politicians and planners, many of whom have been unaware of their responsibilities in this sector.

If we wish to look at this in a little more detail in specific relation to the UK, we need to study the workings of companies that use their own aircraft for executive travel. The members of the Business Aircraft Users Association generate more than £20,000 million in export earnings annually and provide more than 70,000 jobs in the UK. Yet they have difficulties in gaining access to the nation's airports and airspace and need to fight for slots in competition with the charter and scheduled operators on their sun-seeking holiday flights.

An element within GA that has received more than its share of unwarranted adverse publicity is the air display movement. This, too, has a role to perform in a wider sphere than its own, for not only does it create and maintain an interest in aviation among a very broad band of the public, but it provides opportunities for people to have their introductions to the air through pleasure flights. Many who travel on airliners would not do so if they had not 'broken the ice' first with local trips round the aerodrome at these events.

Everyone involved with the civil side of flying displays in the UK has been
affected by recent changes in the legislation, calling for organisers to obtain

permission and particularly pilots to acquire 'display authorisations' from the CAA. These requirements came into effect on 1st April 1989 and were introduced because concern had been expressed about the safety of shows. Yet throughout 1988, during which there were more than 650 events at which some form of flying was involved, there was not one accident involving a civil pilot or civil aeroplane at a civil show. Only the Services suffered mishaps, but by complicated political 'discussions' between the Ministry of Defence and the Civil Aviation Authority, the military side is exempt from all the new requirements that allegedly were essential in the pursuit of safety in the world of flying displays.

General aviation has been the target for constant criticism from ill-informed quarters. Whenever a pilot unwittingly penetrates a corner of regulated airspace or makes an unsuccessful forced landing, the media, often abetted by politicians, will take every opportunity to make a verbal snipe at the movement. So it is important to appreciate the size of UK GA and the extent of its activities. The latest available information indicates that this sector flew about 900,000 hours in the past 12 months, compared with about 600,000 by the commercial air transport operators. Internationally it is accepted that for statistical purposes each GA aircraft averages two movements per hour, while for CAT, average stage lengths produce a movement about every two hours. On this basis the smaller operators achieved roughly 1.8 million movements in the year to the CAT figure of about 300,000. As take-off and landing are the most critical of the flight phases, we discover that GA pilots are 'at greater risk' on 6 times more occasions than are the heavier operators. Also, there are many other factors to feed into the calculations, for nearly all the air transport aircraft fly for most of the time in protected airspace, with two professional pilots on board, while the average GA flight is conducted in the funnels and tunnels and other areas that remain available, with a single-pilot operation and, at times, heavy cockpit workloads.

Surely, but not very steadily, the GA movement has enjoyed a progressive reduction in the overall accident rate, with the sole exception of 1987 in which a statistical hiccup occurred. With such a very small sample to use as a measuring stick, the fact that there were 27 fatal accidents in the year is virtually meaningless; yet, predictably the political bells of alarm were pressed in all the customary quarters and the CAA was forced to form its own internal study group, but with no direct participation by the outside organisations that normally are involved in such activities. As a result, a detailed document (CAP 542: General aviation accident review 1987) was generated as an appeasement exercise, but it received a cool reception from people in the field. As an example it contains reference to the possibility of further checks on the competency of private pilots, yet the most glaring information in the whole report is that of the 27 accidents, 7 involved twin-engine aircraft. As in the GA category these account for only about 5 per cent of the total fleet, the figure is disproportionately high. Here, though, is the missing link: the report states that there is no proven need 'to propose adjustment of the monitoring of Aerial Work and Public Transport activities since this is already carefully controlled by the Authority's Flight Operations Inspectorate'. In isolation, fine; but four of the seven twin-engine aircraft involved in these fatal accidents during 1987 were flown by professionals and not by private pilots!

Although one bad year was sufficient to cause alarm, with proposals for drastic changes, in the following year, 1988, GA enjoyed the lowest accident rate since records have been kept. So if one year in isolation is a valid yardstick when the results are poor, now can we reverse the situation and say that because of the safety success in 1988, all proposals in CAP 542 can be abandoned!? For decisions to be credible, the CAA must act one way *or* the other. The movement will not accept judgment based on whatever suits the mood of the moment.

Perhaps, as a change from my own writing, the opinion of one with very special experience in this field will be appropriate. I quote from the pen of R.D. Campbell, mentioned in an earlier chapter in his capacity as Chairman of AOPA UK and Co-ordinator for the European Region of International AOPA:

> The report by the CAA Study Group concerning the higher-than-normal number of fatalities in 1987 is something of a confusing paradox in that:-
>
> a) The Group was unable to assess the amount of increased activity in UK General Aviation, ie the number of movements flown. Without this figure it was impossible to determine whether the fatal accident rate per number of movements was higher, lower or similar to previous years.
> b) The Group's investigations did not unearth any specific major causes for the 1987 increase in the fatal accident rate, nor was any individual factor identified where adjustment would be likely to have a fully satisfactory effect on the achievement of an overall improvement.
> c) The Group further stated in its report that there was 'indeterminate statistical significance' upon which to base its conclusions, adding that the value of additional regulatory measures was felt to be minimal in a quest to improve safety. Then it went further to say that the provision of additional regulation would be irrational and nugatory. Yet its Recommendations contained actions which, if followed through, would cause 6 new Regulations to be formulated. This section of the report also stated that changes to the existing Regulations would make a direct contribution to the reduction of future GA accident rates.

> In studying aviation accidents over a long period it can be seen without doubt that the causes of most accidents are lack of decisions or incorrect decisions. The report touched very lightly on this aspect and came to the conclusion that there was a positive need to improve decision-making ability, yet at the same time no specific suggestions were made as to how this could be achieved. Thus, this most important item does not appear in the Group's Recommendations. Whilst appreciating that the subject of training pilots to make good decisions may well have been beyond the expertise of the Group, some positive results would have been achieved if the Group had taken the trouble to consult with experts from the pilot training industry. This, however, was not done, so little, if anything, was achieved by the CAA Study Group in relation to improving the future GA accident rate.

Although GA has suffered its share of criticism from many quarters, we must not overlook the tendency for events in the USA to work their ways across the Atlantic in our direction and, a few years later, to apply here. So these recent words from Allan McArtor, Administrator of the US Federal Aviation Administration, should be digested by those who have failed to be enlightened:

We've all heard negative talk about Piper Cubs cluttering up the skies – even though those 'Cubs' may be $100,000 high-performance retractables with $25,000 worth of avionics on board.

Misinformed people who talk that way simply haven't thought about it. They haven't realised that general aviation is a national asset. It's not general aviation against the airlines. It's really general aviation *and* the airlines, because general aviation is now our primary source of airline pilots.

Now, for the first time in the history of aviation, we're on the verge of a pilot shortage. In the past few months, airlines have hired pilots in their forties and a couple have hired some over fifty. Can you believe it? So, with the military supply down and the demand up, we're relying on general aviation to provide the training and experience for pilots who will some day move into the left seats of our jetliners.

The only point to add is that, on this occasion, we appear to be ahead of the US, for our airlines have relied on GA for several years and already many of its products are in the captain's seat.

Now back to the central subject of space. In the past, almost all planning has been based on the strengths of the calls from the commercial air transport operators, or, less acceptably, from trade unions, but recent pressures from within the GA movement have made clear that this must stop. The Ministerial directions to the CAA and NATS are equally clear in stating that the needs of all users, including GA, must be taken into account, which clearly is as it should be, for by its sheer size this sector must have more space in which to operate if safety is not to be seriously degraded. This extends beyond just airspace, essential though that is, for there is an apparently increasing level of misunderstanding among some airport operators about the essential part that GA contributes to the total aviation scene. Indirectly every airport and aerodrome is partially dependent on GA for its long-term viability, but we will uncover that in the next chapter.

I end this section with a reference to scale: in 1988, more general aviation aircraft were *added* to the UK register than the *total* number of airliners on the combined fleets of all the UK air transport operators! Few people engaged in any branch of civil aviation can afford to ignore that.

Chapter 12
Where is all
this Air Traffic?

HEATHROW IS the world's busiest international airport. So we hear over and over again. This is a good promotional message and no-one can blame those who use it as an excuse to cover the problems of crowded terminals, handling delays and, of course, congested airspace; but if we remove the word *international,* we see the UK's main airport in its true position in the real world.

All distances within Britain are reasonably short and, as the mainland has acceptably good rail and road facilities, these are, and always will be, the main travel modes. UK domestic air services carry fewer passengers in a year than British Rail moves each single working weekday, so in number terms internal air transport movements can be virtually discounted. So, by virtue of our geographical position as an island, nearly all UK air traffic is international. A movement is a movement, so whether it arrives in the UK after about 220 miles from Paris or in the USA it has covered 2000 miles across that continent is totally irrelevant, except that the first is entitled to the magic word 'international'. The only difference concerns the space and facilities required for customs and immigration purposes, but in terms of runway or airspace requirements an airliner is an airliner, regardless of origin or destination.

So now we look down the lists of the world's busiest airports in terms of total commercial air transport movements, based on the latest information available through the International Civil Aviation Organisation (ICAO). We study the 'top ten', but alas, Heathrow is not there. However, we find it in thirteenth place, so while we are thumbing through the data we decide to seek where Gatwick stands in the status sheets. Unfortunately, though, only the busiest 25 appear on the list and Gatwick has failed to gain a place in the pop charts. As with Heathrow, it features in terms of international movements, but for the reasons that I have given this is meaningful only for purposes of publicity. It is no measure of the comparative scale of aviation activity in and around the airport.

By now many readers will have realised the importance of the points that I am pressing, but as this information forms the core of the reason for this book, perhaps a few embellishments will make the picture even more clear-cut. To find a busy airport we need to look at activities in the United States, where Atlanta (Hartfield) and Chicago (O'Hare) have some very impressive movement figures. *Each* of these alone handles about 30 per cent more commercial air transport

movements than the *combined* efforts of Heathrow, Gatwick, Luton, Stansted and

London City. What is perhaps more important, though, is that despite the intensity of air traffic in the States, this is not used as an excuse for endless delays. Last year, of all flights by the 13 largest airlines at the 27 busiest airports, 80.5 per cent landed within 15 minutes of their scheduled times. Perhaps we could stop this chapter at this point and send our airspace planners to their drawing boards to dismantle the complex and 'bitty' set-up that they have managed to generate in the London area. By world standards we have much to learn and if still we talk about a need to increase the amount of air that is controlled, we must ask ourselves why we have made such a mess of the existing situation when our traffic figures are so modest.

Quite independently, two pilots who fly regularly into and out of Heathrow have described the unbelievable ground movements that occur. One drew a diagram of his route from Terminal 4, *across* the southern runway (09R/27L) for a take-off on 09L. Then there are tales of aircraft being towed about, causing delays to 'live' machines, partly because of failure by the tug drivers to understand radio phraseology and procedures. No great effort would be needed to insist that anyone operating on the active area is required to have suitable training. One contributor said that many of the delays and much of the congestion must be put down to a 'lack of co-ordination of who is doing what, where and when'.

If London fails to feature among the places with really busy airspace and heavy traffic, when we move our minds to the provinces we wonder why air travel, not only within but to and from the UK, is such a small-scale activity. The figures are shattering in terms of their relative insignificance. I make no apology for my frequent comparisons between figures for air and rail, for in transport terms each is no more than a people-mover and, as such, must be judged on its merits in terms of space required, inconvenience caused to others, pollution produced, speed with which congestion is cleared and all the other norms of comparison. So here, to give balance to the scene we stay within the UK. After Heathrow, Gatwick, Manchester and Glasgow, Birmingham has the highest passenger throughput of any UK airport. In October 1988 a claim was publicised because an all-time record figure of 362,278 people had been handled in the previous *month*. Within a few days I learned that 470,000 passengers arrive at Waterloo station between 7 and 10 a.m. on *each working weekday* throughout the year. We complain about BR's timekeeping as more of a habit than as a proven fact, so I was very interested to read a recent report from the Central Transport Consultative Committee with their figures showing that, nationally throughout the UK, 90 per cent of trains arrive at their destinations no more than 5 minutes late. This may not be good enough, but it shows our strange attitudes towards what we expect from different quarters. We *expect* aeroplanes to be late; we *complain* when trains are. To add weight to this I mention a comment in the *Guardian* on 16th June 1988, which read 'Manchester Airport was almost back to normal. Delays in general were limited to four hours'.

I should add that in making these comments about two of our leading provincial airports I am not doing so to criticise either of those places individually. I am quoting these figures and remarks to provide general evidence in support of the case. In practice, Birmingham Airport has a very enlightened management with an encouragingly constructive outlook and only the obstructiveness of an external Government agency has prevented completion of a special terminal for GA users. Many other airports, most of which handle minimal commercial traffic, could do well to learn from Birmingham.

This leads me into those other airports. Nearly all operated for many years as general aviation aerodromes to serve the needs of their localities. There were no restrictions on who could use them and when, nor were there any complicated procedures for arrivals or departures. Pilots were expected to 'do their own things' and cope, keeping their eyes and ears open and their minds switched on. Since then, progressively but apparently interminably, some of these places have sought to impose restrictions on the majority of users and I could write many pages of tales about these unfortunate attitudes that are developing. There are several stories of training aircraft being 'held' for up to 20 minutes away from base to allow one commercial air transport movement to trundle in for many miles; a tale of a beacon being switched off when a GA pilot was in the midst of an instrument let down, with a one-minute warning of 'we close at 6'; an airport manager asked me if I 'could stop these flying schools and clubs sending their students to my place on their cross-countries, because they foul-up the system and get in the way of the real pilots'; a report from the same airport at which the controller asked the pilot of a Service Chipmunk to clear the ATZ because another light aeroplane – the only other machine in the circuit – had intermittent transmitter trouble; and the airport that refused permission for the pilot of a light twin to land on the into-wind runway because it was being used for a cadet parade. He was faced with the choice of landing in conditions that exceeded the aircraft's cross-wind limits or to divert; his passengers were not impressed. These should suffice as samples.

You may ask why I have included these tales of woe in a chapter devoted to the amounts of traffic handled in the UK. The reason is to express concern for the future on two separate counts. Firstly, the uncharitable attitudes come mainly from a new generation of airport managements and controllers who have no experience of the ways in which civil aviation operated in earlier and happier years. Secondly, if, with such small amounts of commercial traffic and when handling so few passengers, these places are proving incapable of coping with GA aircraft, what will happen if – as some predict – air travel *does* expand to become a major transporter of people? Will GA need to move to smaller aerodromes and, if so, will such facilities be available? This is a key question that must be answered, for as I made clear in the preceding chapter, general aviation is an essential component in the system if civil aviation is to expand into the twenty-first century.

Unfortunately, partly for geographical reasons, Britain is not an air-orientated nation and our present attitudes will act as severe constraints on the chances of successful expansion. Only one in 2500 Britons holds a pilot's licence, whereas in The USA the ratio is 1 in 565. But how will we learn to manage *if* our air traffic does increase? Again we will need to take lessons from the USA, where all airports except one accept general aviation aircraft to mix in large numbers with the very substantial quantity of commercial traffic. In any real expansion, our present totally restrictive outlook – not just in terms of CAT/GA allocations but even in CAT terms alone – will be totally untenable.

If there *is* much air activity over the UK, is it all where it should be? We hear constant cries about congestion in the London area, yet equally the provincial airports point out that they are prevented from expanding to their full potentials by numerous outside influences, not the least of which is the Government. To take full-page advertisements in national newspapers, Manchester must have meant what it claimed with its statement that one million passengers wish to fly between there and the USA in a year, yet licence restrictions prevented more than 80,000 travelling from their chosen airport. The remainder needed to travel from

Q. 1 million people want to fly direct from Manchester to America. What's to stop them?

A. Ask the Government.

Q Over 1 Million people would have found it easier to fly direct from Manchester to the U.S.A.*

So why could Manchester Airport serve only 80,000 of them?

A ASK THE GOVERNMENT.

Q The London Airports offer 400 scheduled flights a week to America. Manchester is limited to 16.**

When licence applications to increase the Manchester services were put to the Department of Transport by American Airlines, Northwest and Pan Am they were refused. Why?

A ASK THE GOVERNMENT.

Q The 920,000 who cannot fly from Manchester had to waste time and money travelling through the South because they were forced to use the already congested London airports.

What is the reasoning behind perpetuating the overload problem in the South by restricting expansion elsewhere?

A ASK THE GOVERNMENT.

Q The Government recognises that Airports act as prime centres of economic recovery within the regions. Direct long-haul routes not only offer existing companies an opportunity to expand into foreign markets but also act as a magnet to attract overseas investors. Why deprive the North of this potential?

A ASK THE GOVERNMENT.

Q Why did the Government state in the 1985 White Paper that 'Airports should be free to compete as far as possible and provide the necessary facilities... to enable Airlines to meet demand when and where it arises' and then ignore the Airlines' plea that such demand exists at Manchester?

A ASK THE GOVERNMENT.

Q What do 20 Million people living in an area best served by Manchester Airport have to do to get the services they need from an Airport committed to providing them?

A ASK THE GOVERNMENT.

*1 million passengers flying between Manchester and America. Department of Employment International Passenger survey 1986
**Summer Schedules 1988

MANCHESTER AIRPORT
BRITAIN'S CENTRAL GATEWAY
MANCHESTER AIRPORT plc   MANCHESTER M22 5PA UK   TEL 061 489 3000

Manchester Airport's cri de coeur *which appeared in the national newspapers.*

London and add to any congestion problems that might exist. Manchester's plea is published in full on the preceding page.

Although in terms of scale Manchester's problem is very significant, it is not alone. Airports all over the country claim that they are under-used and are prevented from fulfilling their intended roles. At the reopening ceremony for Blackpool's main runway in 1988, the Airport's Managing Director made many pointed comments: 'Blackpool Airport is a greatly under-valued and under-used facility. . . . However, that role could be vastly increased to everyone's benefit . . . but being well equipped is rather pointless if there are insufficient customers. The airport has been working hard to encourage additional passengers on scheduled services, has been exploring the possibility of new scheduled routes and encouraging tour operators and airlines to run charters out of the airport.' So, although the reason for Blackpool's shortage of business is based on a different premise from that of Manchester, the problem is identical: grossly under-used airports. Not surprisingly, a policy statement to central Government issued by the Joint Airports Committee of Local Authorities (JACOLA) included 'Urgent steps must be taken to ensure that the airline industry does not operate in such a way as to frustrate the ability of passengers to fly from the nearest airport whenever it is commercially viable to do so'.

The problem of spreading the load among all the available airports is not restricted to the north. Shoreham Airport near Brighton has put forward several suggestions for operators to launch their south-heading services from there, while Kent International has made justifiable claims that its services are cheaper than those of Gatwick, adding 'KIA also offers the huge safety bonus of being outside the London Terminal Manoeuvring area, which avoids congestion and delays, both inbound and outbound'. How refreshingly encouraging to hear a commercial operator stressing the benefits of being *outside* the over-protected TMA.

Scotland, too, has its problems and in January 1989 BAA asked the Government to initiate an immediate review of its policy for the distribution of air traffic in the Lowlands. Under the Airports Act 1986, with limited exceptions the Traffic Distribution Rules for Scotland prohibit any commercial air traffic to or from points outside Europe from using either Glasgow or Edinburgh Airports. In an attempt to justify the continued use of Prestwick as the designated gateway for long haul services to and from Scotland, these restrictions remain in force and prevent people from travelling to and from the airports nearest their homes. Prestwick's performance as an international airport has been dismal, but when the British Aerospace flying college began operations there recently, giving the airport a renewed purpose in terms of increased movements, the controllers were unable or unwilling to handle the extra traffic and many of the training flights were transferred to Cumbernauld, where new conflicts arose with low-flying RAF traffic. ('Take it away from me. Give it to someone else . . .')

The regional problems have not escaped discussion in either Houses of Parliament and in the upper house on 30th November 1988 Lord Gainford asked what measures the Government was taking to encourage growth of these airports. Lord Brabazon, Under Secretary of State, Department of Transport replied 'My Lords, the 1985 Airports Policy White Paper noted that regional airports have a role to play in relieving the pressure on London airports and it expressed the Government's concern to encourage their growth and development. We accordingly provide special borrowing allocations for municipal airports whose expansion is justified; and we continue, both in the EC and in bilateral negotiations, to pursue policies of liberalisation in order to maximise the scope for regional air services'. In reply to a further question, Lord Brabazon stated 'The regional airports are growing and have grown very strongly over the past few years. Unfortunately, the air traffic control problems affect regional airports as much as the London airports'. His words, however, conflict with the pleas from the people who run these airports and his point about air traffic control cannot apply if these places are as under-used as they appear to be.

Lord Mason of Barnsley's point made later in the same discussion is worthy of publication almost in full: 'My Lords, is the Minister aware that tour operators impose a supplement on fares for those who travel abroad from regional airports? This deters families from travelling from provincial airports and adds to the congestion at Gatwick. For example, a supplement from Manchester to Majorca is between £40 and £50 per person . . . unfair to northerners . . . an extra burden on the provincial airports . . . if that deterrent were removed the congestion at Gatwick would be quickly eased.' To this Lord Brabazon replied, surprisingly, 'It is possible that the handling charges at the regional airports are more expensive than those at Gatwick and Heathrow'. Less surprisingly, the noble Lords rejected that answer outright.

Clearly the problem is far from solved and there is little evidence that the political will exists to balance the load. We have under-used airports and generous areas of available airspace in almost all parts of Britain and yet we fail to tackle any of the related problems at their roots. Perhaps a few figures for passengers at various airports in September 1988 may be eye-openers. I have selected this month as it gives a representatively fair picture, for it is neither a peak nor a trough in the annual traffic pattern:

Heathrow	3,637,000
Gatwick	2,342,000
Birmingham	362,278
Newcastle	185,321
East Midlands	166,062
Aberdeen	147,200
Stansted	135,600
Leeds/Bradford	72,649
Prestwick	40,500
Teesside	34,258
Exeter	21,656

So it is very clear to see where the commercial air traffic is, but when we transfer this into movements (and a movement is a take-off *or* a landing, so each arrival and departure counts for two) we see more clearly the scale of the UK operation. Samples of commercial air transport movements for the same month are:

Heathrow	28,400
Gatwick	17,600
Glasgow	5,600
Newcastle	5,186
East Midlands	3,118
Stansted	2,200
Leeds/Bradford	1,896
Teesside	1,386
Exeter	771
Prestwick	400

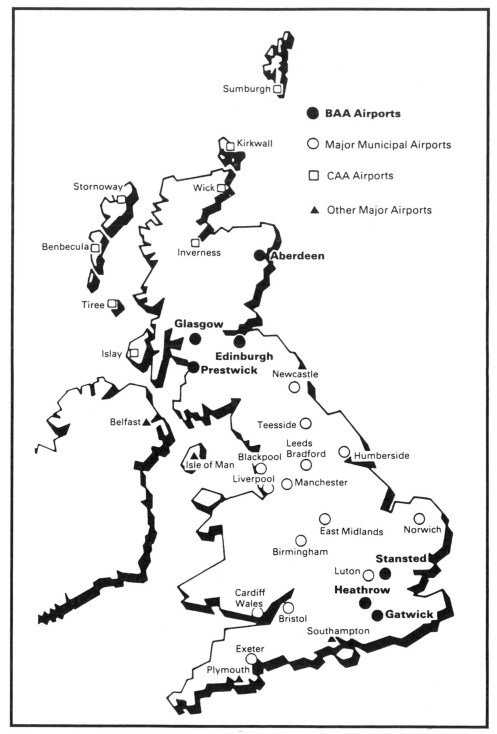

Sumburgh

● **BAA Airports**

○ Major Municipal Airports

□ CAA Airports

▲ Other Major Airports

Kirkwall

Stornoway

Wick

Benbecula

Inverness

Aberdeen

Tiree

Glasgow

Islay

Edinburgh
Prestwick

Newcastle

Belfast ▲

Teesside

Leeds
Bradford

Humberside

Blackpool

Isle of Man

Liverpool

Manchester

East Midlands

Norwich

Birmingham

Stansted

Luton

Heathrow

Cardiff
Wales

Bristol

Gatwick

Southampton ▲

Exeter

Plymouth ▲

100 *Major airports in the UK. (Courtesy National Economic Development Office).*

This information has been provided by the airports, but sometimes it is difficult to find figures that are directly comparable, for I discovered that one airport was counting Bulldog light trainers of a University Air Squadron as 'commercial movements'! Others are more realistic in their calculations. Several of these places reported reductions in holiday charter traffic in 1988 compared with 1987, which is a factor that makes a nonsense of many press reports and is a project worth watching for the future.

What we need to do now is to see what all this means in terms of traffic density. An analysis carried out at Teesside during one week in November 1988 showed that, taking the published opening hours of 0700-2130 daily, over seven days, the average was 1.69 scheduled movements per hour, or considerably less than one landing and one take-off per hour. This, of course, was not at a peak time of the year, but schedules tend to be less seasonably variable than other flights so it provides some helpful information.

Most people consider that most movements in the UK – or for that matter, anywhere – are commercial air traffic. Therefore it is logical to assume that the airports are the busiest places in terms of traffic counts. To obtain direct comparisons we need to go back to the calendar year 1987, for which some very useful research was carried out by the Aerodrome Owners Association. This, coupled with statistics produced by the CAA and published in CAP 536 (UK Airports 1987) can be united to produce some interesting facts: the general aviation aerodrome at Wycombe Air Park (Booker) handled more movements than Manchester International Airport; the private aerodrome at Blackbushe handled more movements than Luton; Oxford and Cranfield each moved more aircraft than Birmingham.

Then, to give comparison of scale, we should look at a random sample of airports and larger aerodromes to check the number of air transport movements against the total figures:

	Total Movements	Air Transport Movements
Aberdeen	91,331	66,843
Birmingham	76,103	51,564
Blackpool	67,645	8,516
Bournemouth	79,111	6,116
Bristol	53,408	11,141
Coventry	63,197	532
Dundee	38,306	1,906
East Midlands	62,897	29,515
Exeter	50,260	8,935
Gatwick	189,202	173,828
Gloucester/Cheltenham	57,117	441
Heathrow	329,977	308,031
Inverness	21,239	5,973
Leeds/Bradford	41,770	16,465
Liverpool	74,069	18,405
Prestwick	42,674	3,900
Shoreham	57,794	347
Swansea	14,475	589
Teesside	57,455	10,815

So from this list we see vast variation between places such as Heathrow and Gatwick, where almost all movements fall into the CAT category, and Coventry, Gloucester/Cheltenham (Staverton)and Shoreham where such commercial activity is little more than 1 per cent of the total. This does not complete the picture, however, for of a total of 136 licensed airports and aerodromes in the UK, only 25 can claim 10,000 or more air transport movements in the year; and even this figure amounts to only 13 take-offs and 13 landings in each period of 24 hours.

A relevant feature in all this is that in many cases the airports with the smallest numbers of CAT movements are the ones that tend to become protective about their surrounding airspace. The airport manager mentioned earlier who had asked for student pilots not to be sent to his place was on poor ground, for commercial air transport accounted for fewer than 10 per cent of his year's movements, so without substantial GA traffic it would have been a sadly forsaken area of inactivity.

As I have mentioned several times, GA is the largest sector of all aviation activity and many of its aerodromes handle traffic that would put the air transport world to shame. On one day in July 1988 the small grass aerodrome at Stapleford in Essex handled 3,014 movements and a few days later the famous motor racing track at Silverstone attracted 3,068 movements. These, of course, are special peak figures and are not repeated regularly, but if we care to multiply by the days in the year, in each case we would reach a figure well in excess of a million. I mention this because in capacity terms if this traffic can be accepted in one day it *could* be practicable on others. Heathrow's average daily movement figure is little more than 800, and although frequently we hear about limits on runway capacity, a peak/trough graph produced in the summer of 1988 and published in *The Daily Telegraph* showed that the *actual* use failed to reach capacity at any time; at Gatwick the capacity/use gap was larger than that at Heathrow for most of the average day, but the lines touched at one point in the morning peak. The problem is that many booked slots are not used, either because the airline concerned has endeavoured to operate to a hopelessly tight schedule and is not ready for departure, or because a machine has gone early (yes, this has been known!) and the booked slot has not been re-allocated by the airport.

Another case of the small numbers of aircraft and passengers handled concerns a statement that appeared in *The Times* on 25 July 1988. Under the heading 'AIR TRAVEL DELAYS AVERAGE THREE HOURS' we read: ' A CAA spokesman said "We have coped reasonably well with what was probably the busiest weekend of the year." At Gatwick, one of the world's busiest airports (*sic*), where nearly 50,000 people passed through the North Terminal this weekend, a spokesman said "We were quite pleased with the way things went."'

There cannot be any other bulk-moving traffic mode that considers 50,000 people to be a large number for a whole weekend. Already I have made embarrassing comparisons with British Rail figures, but for a change let us look at roads. A dual 3-lane motorway can have a design capacity for up to 85,000 vehicles in a day of 16 hours, so if we take the standard figure of 2.5 occupants in a car, we have a practical movement potential, without any crowding or congestion, of considerably more than 200,000 people in that time. If you feel that my continual comparisons with less demanding travel modes are unfair, let us revert to matching like with like; a graph in the *Financial Times* for 26 August 1988 revealed numbers of CAT aircraft handled in 1987. The top 22 airports in the USA coped with 10.2 million movements, but in Europe the busiest 42 between them managed only 5.6 m. So again we need to look across the Atlantic if we wish to see high levels of activity.

To describe the situation is one matter, but to provide solutions is another. Without doubt the problems revolve largely around attitudes and outlooks (or in some cases, I fear, inlooks). Some years ago when two or three aerodromes changed their titles to airports, the complex caught on, and one by one, more followed. Not to be outdone, some added boosts to their falling ego by adding the word 'international' to the name. As I have explained already, almost all UK schedules and all holiday flights are international, so almost any aerodrome that has an occasional service can claim to be an 'international airport'. It may be significant that the smaller the volume of traffic the more important is the name, for the places that essentially are international have no need to boost their confidence by their titles: who has heard of Heathrow International or Gatwick International?

While in itself a name may not be important in a broader context, in practice this tendency has led to the introduction of what could be called restrictive practices. Some airports have used very strange methods (think back to the RAF Bulldog story) to endeavour to establish their levels of commercial activity and, sometimes on such spurious calculations, have hoodwinked NATS to agree to the introduction of their own chunks of regulated airspace. This has been the subject of severe criticism from the GA movement. No-one in his senses wishes to fly a light private aeroplane round the circuit at Heathrow and it is perfectly reasonable that he should not be permitted to do so, but when we see the abysmal traffic figures relating to most regional airports, we see also a strong need for the managements and controllers at such places to remove their blinkers. Do they *really* believe that they are busy and cannot accommodate the majority of would-be GA users? It seems strange that on the one hand they call to the Government (and to anyone who may listen) that they are under-used, short of schedules and not permitted to provide the services sought by their local residents, then at the same time show a total disinterest in the scope for expanding their general aviation activities and therefore help to establish more stable long-term futures. We have seen the diminished fortunes of more than one airport that thrived for a few years on a small handful of schedules and, when airline operators withdraw, the places deteriorated because they had been geared to the wrong economic values. Recently I was told by the Assistant Director of one such place that he was about to leave his job because his Director had great ideas about concentrating on scheduled services. He described this as pie in the sky which almost certainly would lead to the aerodrome's downfall. He wanted to go before that happened. Another such 'airport' is the subject of repeated rumours about likely closure; but *before* the schedules began, it had operated satisfactorily as a GA aerodrome, which it could be doing happily today. . . .

Of course there are a few areas of the UK in which there is some fairly intense activity; however, in the main this is not because of the overall amount of flying, but because operations are restricted to small gaps between large portions of controlled airspace and often at very restricted heights. The country's worst example of this – typifying some *very* bad planning – is the south-east sector of the London Terminal Manoeuvring Area. Already I have mentioned the problems caused by the handful of flights from London City Airport and hurriedly-introduced measures taken to accept these into airspace that is needed by a much larger number of other users; effectively this has lowered the standards of safety for those operators who are compelled to contain their activities into a 103 far smaller volume of airspace than before. The airline concerned has admitted carrying only 58,000 passengers in the year between London City and Paris and the demand for this will diminish drastically when the Channel Tunnel comes into use. Yet GA generates 200,000 movements each year in that area and many of these are essential flights for pilot training and business purposes. On loadings of only 2.5 people in each GA machine, this means that the *convenience* of fewer than 60,000 people takes precedence over the *safety* of half a million. All these GA movements could be accommodated happily – and with space to spare – if they could spread their activities into a sensible and practical airspace allocation. Unfortunately, though, NATS has weakened under politically-backed commercial and other pressures and has allowed a few people's greed to take precedence over a large number's need.

Many GA organisations have expressed their concern over this particularly inept arrangement and these have been placed on written record. An example from one of the leading representative bodies is in a news release issued in January 1989, which ends with: 'In a continuing campaign for increased safety, the Aircraft Owners and Pilots Association of the UK has repeated the warning that the present proposals constitute a recipe for danger, so in the event of a mid-air collision or other accident to a general aviation aircraft the Association will make plain to the media where the responsibility rests'.

Yet, despite the warnings from users and with only minimal adjustment to the original plans, the added constraints were placed upon pilots in the Spring of 1989. This is not the first occasion on which such unwise moves have been made and, jointly, the movement has been forced to involve the International Civil Aviation Organisation (ICAO) on grounds of discrimination against GA in contravention of the terms of the Chicago Convention. This is being processed as the book closes for press. Also, approaches have been made to the E.C.

When I showed a first draft of this chapter to one of the many experienced airspace users who are keeping a check on my writings, he offered a most practical suggestion. He compared our alleged airspace/runway congestion position with Britain's inability to cope with snow. Each time we have a few inches of this, he said, our transport and communications systems suffer an instant seizure, as though it is the first occasion on which snow has fallen in the UK, whereas countries that have learnt to live with regular falls plan ahead and cope. His comparison with the air was that we have lived for so long without any pressures on our underused airspace and airports that even the small percentage activity increase of recent years has revealed the short-comings of both the planning and management of our commercial aviation affairs.

There are a few times and places even in Britain at which considerable numbers of aircraft congregate, but certainly not at our 'international' airports. The Popular Flying Association's annual rally at Cranfield in Bedfordshire attracts the biggest assembly of aeroplanes and in recent years attendances have topped the 1000 mark. The most frequently expressed comment heard about this occasion is that the rally should be a compulsory study visit for all NATS controllers and for all air traffic trainees, so that when they return to their normal tasks they can be thankful for the relatively empty skies that they are required to monitor. However, if Cranfield is busy by our parochial standards, again we need to look further afield to the United States if we are to find aviation happening in really large doses.

For this I refer to the Experimental Aircraft Association's Annual Convention at Oshkosh and I am indebted to John Thorpe, Head of the CAA's Safety

To see large numbers of aeroplanes we need to turn to General Aviation. This gathering of light aircraft was at the Popular Flying Association's annual rally some years ago. Today it is not unusual to see over 1000 aircraft at such an event, a substantial number of them arriving in absolute safety without being radio-fitted. (Photo Gordon Bain)

Promotion Section, for information based on first-hand experience of this unique event. On the following page you will see a copy of the arrival procedures. Read these very carefully and take on board what *can* be done to handle very large numbers of aircraft of varying sizes and speeds. More than 15,000 aircraft attended the most recent convention and 2,100 of these participated in the displays or flypasts. The best way to absorb it all though, is to read this report written by John Thorpe;

Air Traffic At Oshkosh Airshow

The Oshkosh Airshow becomes for 10 days at the end of July and the beginning of August every year, the busiest airfield in the world with up to 15,000 visiting aircraft. Interspaced amongst these are the scheduled service DC9s. For arriving light aircraft, there are very special procedures and it is all on a no response system; you do what you are told and say nothing. Whilst listening to the tannoy which was tuned into the frequency, I heard somebody in a light aircraft trying to talk to the ground controllers. His radio was intermittent and the ground controllers said 'the blue Cherokee with the bad radio turn left over the lake, go someplace else and get your radio fixed, we don't want you here'. As I watched I saw the aircraft turn away over the lake and disappear from sight. I also one evening shared a taxi with a couple who

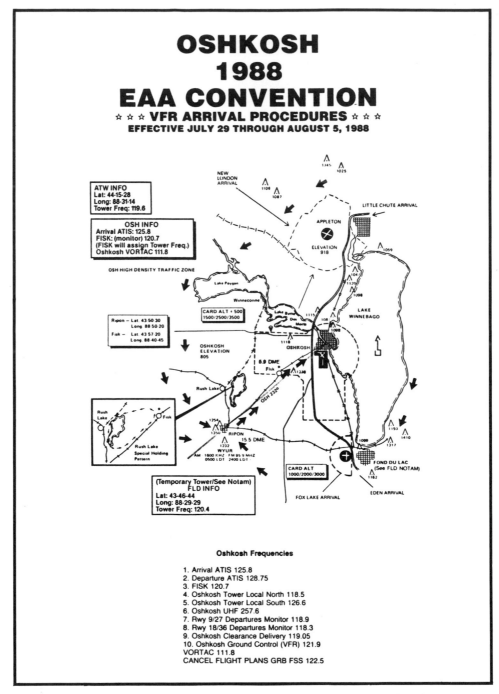

OSHKOSH 1988 EAA CONVENTION
☆ ☆ ☆ VFR ARRIVAL PROCEDURES ☆ ☆ ☆
EFFECTIVE JULY 29 THROUGH AUGUST 5, 1988

ATW INFO
Lat: 44-15-28
Long: 88-31-14
Tower Freq: 119.6

OSH INFO
Arrival ATIS: 125.8
FISK: (monitor) 120.7
(FISK will assign Tower Freq.)
Oshkosh VORTAC 111.8

OSH HIGH DENSITY TRAFFIC ZONE

Ripon — Lat: 43 50 30
Long: 88 50 20
Fisk — Lat: 43 57 20
Long: 88 40 45

CARD ALT + 500
1500/2500/3500

OSHKOSH
ELEVATION
805

6.9 DME
Fisk

Rush Lake

Rush Lake
Special Holding
Pattern

OSH 233°

1254
1350 RIPON
1232 15 5 DME
WYUR
AM 1600 KHZ FM 95 9 MHz
0500 LDT 2400 LDT

(Temporary Tower/See Notam)
FLD INFO
Lat: 43-46-44
Long: 88-29-29
Tower Freq: 120.4

CARD ALT
1000/2000/3000
(See FLD NOTAM)

NEW LONDON ARRIVAL

LITTLE CHUTE ARRIVAL

APPLETON
ELEVATION 918

LAKE WINNEBAGO

OSHKOSH

FOND DU LAC

FOX LAKE ARRIVAL

EDEN ARRIVAL

Oshkosh Frequencies

1. Arrival ATIS 125.8
2. Departure ATIS 128.75
3. FISK 120.7
4. Oshkosh Tower Local North 118.5
5. Oshkosh Tower Local South 126.6
6. Oshkosh UHF 257.6
7. Rwy 9/27 Departures Monitor 118.9
8. Rwy 18/36 Departures Monitor 118.3
9. Oshkosh Clearance Delivery 119.05
10. Oshkosh Ground Control (VFR) 121.9
VORTAC 111.8
CANCEL FLIGHT PLANS GRB FSS 122.5

Every year the Experimental Aircraft Association's convention at Oshkosh proves that, given discipline and the willingness to 'see and avoid', literally thousands of aircraft can converge in the same airspace without mishap. This chart shows typical Oshkosh approach procedures. (Courtesy Sport Aviation) had flown in in an Aztec and I asked them how it was with the twin mixing in with all the slower singles and the reply was 'no problem, we did what we were told, but somebody didn't and he got sent to the back of the queue'. This is the way that they operate there and in fact on the main arrival runway they get people in short and long and left and right and very often you hear the command 'vacate the runway fast as another guy right behind you'. One evening I visited the tower to see what it was like from their point of view. The main rush after the day's airshow had already departed and things were relatively quiet; in fact the wind was such that they were using the airshow runway for some of the departures. An Aztec had started and was taxying from a point where he could readily make a downwind take-off with only a very slight tailwind on the main airshow runway. He called the tower and requested permission to take off on that runway; they cleared him to do so and asked him to expedite an immediate left turn-out *en route* to his destination to Chicago because there was a DC9 on a 5 mile final on a reciprocal runway. The tower then called the DC9 and said 'you'll see lights coming towards you, it's a light twin, he'll be expediting an immediate turn-out'. I somehow couldn't see this sort of thing happening at a UK airfield; however, because at Oshkosh both the DC9 and the Aztec knew exactly what was going on and why, it really was no problem at all and this demonstrated their flexibility. Another nice feature at Oshkosh is that they have three separate circuits operating; basically there is one runway which is the arrival and departure runway for both light aircraft and for the scheduled DC9s, there is another runway with its own circuit, which is the flyby and airshow runway and before you can use it for a flyby, you must have had a briefing and the briefings are split into groups of speed bands. This means that between for example, 11 and 11.30, it's for aircraft that like a speed range of 60 to 110 knots and then the next half hour will be the faster aircraft; that way you don't get too much overtaking going on. People when they have been briefed are given a coloured card to show they've been briefed and the different colours denote the different speeds bands. There is a marshaller at the point where people turn out onto the runway, who checks to see that people have the cards and they are the appropriate colour. In addition to these two circuits there is in one corner a small microlight circuit and people there were staying within close distance of the circuit and operating quite happily in the same airspace as the people in the flyby pattern who of course were separated from them. There have been mid-air collisions at Oshkosh but, surprisingly, they have been at times when the place has been relatively quiet. Incidentally, the briefing board at Oshkosh has a nice bottom line. It says 'don't do nothing dumb'. That really says it all.

Read the arrival procedure again and re-read the report; and note that this is not just a large collection of light aircraft, as DC-9s on scheduled air transport services are phased happily into the pattern. Note especially the air traffic comment advising the airline captain not to worry about the lights coming toward him in the opposite direction on the runway that he was approaching! If in Britain we cannot bring ourselves to quite such enlightened levels of activity, we have very far to go before we can use the word 'busy' as being appropriate to any of our airports or any of our airspace.

The American approach to *using* aeroplanes and airports must have a far healthier future than the feelings portrayed on the 'Straight and Level' page in *Flight International* dated 29th October 1988. This short piece says almost all that I have endeavoured to put over in this chapter. It appears under a photograph of one person in an otherwise deserted control tower overlooking an empty aerodrome. I promise that I was not the author!

Air traffic control breakdowns

Hello, this is Provincial International Airport. Is that the Minister of Aluminium Clouds? I'm on my third cup of coffee, I've read today's newspaper hysteria about crowded skies and broken ATC computers and I've done the crossword.

I've also just been reading a statement by the director of Manchester Airport that 40 per cent of airline passengers flying into London really want to go to the provinces. May I add that when people or parcels around here want to go abroad, they have to go from London?

Tell the airlines? We can't got hold of them because they're all at Heathrow meetings about departure slots and higher landing fees. When we do get hold of them, they just say we have to be market-oriented.

Hang on, I think I see an aircraft. Oh, it's only some GA rubbish. Send us airliners, Minister. Not too many – we don't want our controllers having nervous breakdowns.

(With acknowledgment and full appreciation to Flight International.)

Chapter 13
Whose is the Problem?

CONTINUALLY we hear that there are various problems affecting commercial air transport operators in and over the UK, but as each section of the aviation community has devoted more time and energy to protecting its own position than in seeking solutions – usually by trying to deflect attention from its own quarter into someone else's pitch – we may find difficulty in identifying where the real problems lie. In a box beside my desk I have an ever-increasing pile of documents produced by various bodies (usually the CAA, but others, too, seem to need to follow this practice) and within the past 18 months or so these have been generated at a rate quite unknown in previous years. Each endeavours to explain what a particular organisation or department is doing to ensure that there is no guilt in that quarter, but we need no degrees in psychology or psychiatry to know the root reasons for tactics such as these.

For the facts we need to look a little more deeply into what is happening in *reality*. Only a modicum of research is needed to unearth individual behaviour patterns, so this chapter contains more of the sayings and writings of other people than my own views and experiences, for only when we assemble the tragic tales of discord can we determine the extent to which self-defence takes precedence over either safety or efficiency.

Firstly we will look at the extent of the liaison, co-operation and understanding that exists between the various bodies concerned; we find that the present round of trouble started in the Spring of 1988, when the CAA anticipated the attacks that it would be receiving from the industry by endeavouring to escape from responsibility. An article headed 'CAA lays it on the line for Government' in *Travel News* dated 29th April states the Authority's claim that 'only the Government has the power to save Britain's air transport system from being totally overwhelmed' and 'the CAA places the ball in the Government's court'. Not surprisingly, however, not long passed before the bricks were flying, and by 10th May *The Times* carried a report 'Airline warns MPs over air traffic control' stating 'British Airways has sent MPs an unpublished memorandum criticising the performance of the Civil Aviation Authority's air traffic control system . . . the system is safe at present, but as it becomes increasingly inefficient, then mistakes occur which in turn lead to concerns over air safety.'

The second half of July in 1988 saw the missiles on the move in rapid-fire mode. For reasons that I mentioned in Chapter 7 I have discounted reports that appeared in the tabloid press, but the events of that time warranted extensive coverage in the 'heavies' and I quote a small sample from literally dozens that appeared.

The first to warrant a mention appeared in *The Independent* on 18th July, under 'CASTING THE BLAME', which went some way to placing the position in balance:

> The holiday companies and government MPs accused the CAA of complacency and incompetence in managing the air traffic control system. The large tour operators *challenged the CAA to produce proof of a travel boom, which, they claimed, had slowed, not grown, this year.*
>
> On several occasions air traffic controllers had said *there was no slot available for three hours for a plane which had already taken off* a spokesman said: 'There is room in the system, which is too inflexible.' (These are my italics, for the industry has received no answer to either of these valid points. D.O.)

Another report in the same issue reported a meeting between Paul Channon, Secretary of State for Transport and Christopher Tugendhat, Chairman of the Civil Aviation Authority:

> Both sides blamed each other. Mr Tugendhat criticised the charter operators for trying to run too many flights with too few aircraft. One airline spokesman accused him of talking nonsense, adding "Mr Tugendhat is arguing that we should operate inefficiently because the air traffic controllers do so" . . . The attacks on Mr Channon intensified speculations that he would be asked to step down from the Cabinet in the next reshuffle . . . The Prime Minister was careful to keep out of the affair yesterday. Downing Street made it clear to the Department that she had no intention of intervening . . .

Now to *The Daily Telegraph* for 22nd July:

> HOLIDAY FLIGHTS DELAYED BY POOR USE OF AIRSPACE. 'Holiday flight delays are due to inefficient use of airspace and the CAA was dishonest in saying it could not accept more flights immediately', Mr Derek Davidson, Chairman of Britannia Airways said yesterday.

and *The Independent* again, also on 22nd July:

> AIRLINE CHIEFS JOIN ATTACK ON CAA. Britain's airlines yesterday condemned the Civil Aviation Authority for its management of air traffic control during this summer's peak period . . . The Chairman of the British Air Transport Association accused the CAA of passing the buck. He was unhappy about the authority's senior management and had made this clear to Paul Channon, the Secretary of State for Transport.
>
> The CAA and the charter airlines disagree on the reasons for the delays, blame each other and even fail to agree on statistics for the growth in flights this summer.
>
> 'There is sufficient airspace if it is used properly' said the Chairman of Britannia, Britain's largest charter airline. 'We're missing flights all the time because of their inefficiency.'

The *Financial Times* for the same date carried a brief report in which the CAA Chairman, Christopher Tugendhat, blamed the airlines for delays, because they were unable to pick-up available slots or take-off allocations as they lacked back-up aircraft and were not able to keep to their own timings.

There were few pauses between the bullets and on 24th July this report appeared in the *Sunday Times:*

> LEAGUE OF SHAME FOR UNPUNCTUAL AIRLINES. The Government has ordered the Civil Aviation Authority to prepare a 'league of shame' to expose the airlines which make passengers wait longest at airports . . . with the aim of embarrassing the worst performers into improving their services. The CAA has told Paul Channon, the Transport Secretary, that chaos is caused largely by charter companies operating on tight margins . . . The airlines deny they are to blame for delays. Peter Villa, Chairman of British Island Airways said 'The CAA will be telling us next that the delays are the passengers' fault for wanting to go abroad'.

Here we turn to the House of Commons where on 26th July Paul Channon, Secretary of State for Transport said 'Some airline scheduling has been more than optimistic and on the verge of being foolhardy . . . Tight scheduling must be investigated'.

Now let us move momentarily to the *Travel Trade Gazette* for 28th July:

> The Civil Aviation Authority and the charter airlines are at each others' throats . . . The CAA gives the impression of immense complacency . . . The CAA says that the charter airlines have been rash because they do not have aircraft to back-up their planned services . . . The CAA will huff and puff, the charter airlines will say that everyone is out of step but them and the Government will remain piggy in the middle.

Not only has the aircraft operating industry had its ration of clashes with the CAA, but in July 1988 the Association of British Travel Agents (ABTA) struck at the authority for making tour operators into scapegoats for that summer's airport chaos. At a formal meeting between the two bodies, the CAA's claim that tour operators' greed had led to too many charter flights was angrily rejected by the ABTA president Jack Smith.

I could quote several more pages of battle reports between the CAA and the commercial operating sector, including one in which 'the entire air traffic control system had collapsed because the CAA had too few telephone lines for co-ordinating flights' *(The Independent,* 18th July), but as these form only one of the areas of conflict I move on now to the next line of entrenchment. As target number two I have chosen runways, for here we can see the Civil Aviation Authority and BAA plc (formerly the British Airports Authority) expending their energies on mutual slating in preference to getting together to agree whether there is a problem and, if so, to formulate a solution.

The problem originated many years ago and to start the story at its roots I am indebted to C.A.P. Ellis, Councillor and Founder Member of the Civil Service Aviation Association, who sent me a copy of his previously published paper on airports and airspace. Part of it reads:

> It is unreasonable to demand an extension of controlled airspace when a limiting factor is the inadequate number of runways upon which the delayed

airliners must inevitably land. This shortage more than any other is the one that Government needs to investigate, since it calls into question nothing less than the credibility of Planning as a tool of government. Apart from the strip at City, no additional runways have been laid in the London region for thirty years, a shortage that has its origins in the 1963 report of the Interdepartmental Committee on a Third London Airport, initiated in great haste following a Public Accounts Committee report recommending the disposal of Stansted Airport. Unsurprisingly the Committee favoured Stansted for the Third LAP. Common prudence might have been expected to dictate the need to acquire some operational experience of a Second LAP with its three runways for which Government approval has been sought and granted, before any reliable assessment of the need for a Third LAP was made. In the event, planning blight descended upon many areas of SE England and has yet to be dispersed entirely. If, instead of instituting no fewer than two ineffective public inquiries into the Third LAP, the Government had appointed an enquiry into 'The Failure of BAA to complete the Second LAP', London might have 33 per cent more runway capacity than it has at present.

Although the battle began far in the past, until recently the firing was random and spasmodic; however 1988 saw new pressures, starting in March with an approach from a new quarter when an anonymous report stated that Gatwick's single runway was unsafe because of the amount of traffic that it handled and because of its inadequate length; this report was in the hands of a Sunday newspaper, which refused to allow the authority to see it. The CAA issued a press release rejecting the irresponsible suggestion and, understandably, claimed that it was unable to comment without being able to see the report and identify the alleged 'near accidents'. However, Robert McCrindle, MP, said that it would be irresponsible of the CAA not to take it seriously. This was reported in *The Times,* the *Sunday Times* and the *Guardian,* but no-one commented on the fact that the airport is owned by BAA and not the CAA.

At about the same time, on 11th March, *Airline World* reported, under 'Runway shortage threat to safety', that the Government's dithering over the provision of extra runway capacity in the south-east could lead to a major disaster. This was followed fairly swiftly when on 31st March the *Financial Times* announced the Report of the Committee on Runway Utilisation at Heathrow and Gatwick, which had been set up on instructions from the Department of Transport and which pressed the need for the Government 'as a matter of urgency to consider provision of extra runway capacity in the south-east'.

We move on now to 23rd June, on which day the *Financial Times* reports the BAA's rejection of a second runway at Gatwick to honour a legal agreement with West Sussex County Council. Two months later in a report under 'BAA rejects blame for air delays' *The Independent* states 'BAA, the airports company, has denied that airport congestion and flight delays in Britain were attributable to a lack of runway space at Gatwick and Heathrow . . . and said it was a matter for the Civil Aviation Authority to rectify . . . A BAA spokesman said "There is sufficient runway capacity in the south-east system to cope with demand until the end of the century. Gatwick doesn't need a second runway . . ."

Here, perhaps, an extract from a press release issued by BAA on 7th June is valid. Headed 'BAA calls upon the CAA to ensure airspace capacity is available to meet demand' the release reads:

London's success as the international crossroads of air transport has not happened by chance. BAA has played its part by ensuring the provision of adequate airport capacity and the British airline industry has responded by developing the services' said Sir Norman Payne, Chairman of BAA plc in his evidence to the Transport Select Committee on Air Traffic Control safety today.

The burden now lies with the CAA to ensure that we have the airspace to meet the demand. We need to be assured that the will and the resources necessary to fulfil that task will be forthcoming.

We do not need sudden crisis solutions as there is no sudden crisis. Safety of operation is the overriding priority, but what we do need is the CAA to continue to improve its performance both in terms of management and equipment . . .

Even on an optimistic view of the rate of growth of air traffic, we think it unlikely that new runway capacity, which would itself add to the peak demands on airspace, will be required in the period up to 2000. Full use of the Stansted runway, and the greater use of runways at Heathrow and Gatwick in the less busy periods, coupled with the gradual introduction of larger aircraft should be sufficient to meet the demand until the turn of the century.

More than four months later, speaking to the Chartered Institute of Transport, Sir Norman continued his theme with 'There is no point having another runway at Heathrow or Gatwick, even if one could be provided . . . we therefore look to a steady improvement in the ability of the National Air Traffic Services to provide an adequate service for the passenger arriving and departing from the United Kingdom.' The Seminar was reported in Flight International on 19th November and this went beyond the one-sided angle put by Sir Norman in the BAA press release. The journal mentioned 'The Chairman of BAA has angered airlines by insisting once again that no new runways are needed in the south east until the next century . . . he blamed the Civil Aviation Authority for contributing to the congestion problem.' More importantly, though, the feelings of the industry were expressed when Peter Owen, British Airways' director of operations, 'claimed that more movements could be handled at Gatwick by integrating take-offs and landings, and he sparked speculation that airlines might build their own airport. "If it is the case that we cannot have the capacity we need provided from established means, then I think that, as an industry, we have to look to other means," he said'. At this stage CAA managing director Tom Murphy was pressed to confirm that private facilities could be operated legally so long as the authority was satisfied with the safety arrangements.

At about the same time, Michael Bishop, Chairman of British Midland Airways, proposed requiring a rebate on air traffic control fees following delays in movements. He went further in expressing his disquiet at the present arrangements with NATS/CAA, by suggesting that a new organisation, divorced from the constraints of the Ministry of Defence and the Civil Aviation Authority, should be established to operate air traffic facilities in UK airspace.

Not long lapsed before the Air Transport Users Committee entered the arena. In this body's annual report, published shortly before Christmas, the Committee urged the Department of Transport to commission a technical enquiry on how to make better use of existing runway space in the south of England, but this was faced with the customary BAA response that all was well. However, ATUC was very critical of BAA's entry into the hotel and property market and into city centre retailing, which had 'done nothing to allay the Committee's concern that these investments are a higher priority for the company's capital than serving the passenger'.

As with the continual disagreements between the CAA and the airlines, I could produce more evidence of the battle between BAA and its 'customers'. I will complete this section of the chapter, however, by reporting a statement issued by the CAA on 2nd February 1989, which claims that the Government should plan to have an extra runway in the south-east for wide-body airliners ready by the year 2000. This appears in a consultative document which could create problems for the Government in view of its struggle to promote a 'green' image, but the report states that, without this added facility, from 2005 about 13 million passengers a year 'will be forced either to use distant airports or not fly at all. In the authority's view, it is of considerable importance that work should now proceed planning for the new runway'. The report mentions the possibility of earmarking for expansion another airport in the south-east, with Kent International (Manston) and Bournemouth as suitable candidates for consideration. Away from the London area, Birmingham and East Midlands Airports are expected to handle considerable growths in charter traffic and Birmingham is forecast to become more heavily used than Manchester, which today is Britain's third busiest airport in terms of commercial movements. BAA's response is that 'a report on future options will be published later this year'.

The fighting is far from finished and, following circulation of the consultative document, there has been further speculation within the industry. On 27th February 1989 *The Independent* devoted an entire page to the subject. Among its comments were:

> The Goverment could soon be backing the development of a large new private sector airport in the South-east, competing with BAA which owns Heathrow, Gatwick and Stansted . . . RAF Manston, an under-used air base in north-east Kent, is emerging as the most likely site. There is strong local support for limited expansion because the airport is in one of the South-east's worst unemployment blackspots . . .
>
> . . . BAA has neither the land nor the inclination to start planning a new runway now. It says this can wait . . . the CAA strongly disagrees . . . There is growing pressure from airlines and the CAA to challenge the BAA's monopoly . .
>
> The CAA has been discreetly promoting the notion that a competitor to the BAA is needed . . .
>
> BAA says that if Stansted grew to its maximum possible size with just one runway it would generate 180,000 extra flights. 'That's 20,000 more than (the CAA) will be able to handle after their air traffic control improvements, and yet the CAA want another runway. We say where's the need?' one BAA official said.

Also in this well prepared study of the situation is a section devoted to the north-south divide. In this, Gil Thompson, Chief Executive of Manchester International, is quoted as saying 'There are still more than six million passenger journeys from our catchment area to South-east airports each year because of the lack of some services from Manchester'. Mr Thompson says that 12 per cent of Britons flying to the USA come from the North, yet only 2.5 per cent of all transatlantic flights go from Manchester.

Although most of the inter-faction hostility has been based on whether the problem is about airspace or runway capacity, all is far from well on matters of purely-domestic significance. At one time NATS held a virtual monopoly on providing air traffic services at the major UK airports, including not only those operated by BAA and the CAA but many in the hands of local authorities. Several of the 'regionals', however, chose to seek other sources for these facilities and some contracted with IAL (formerly International Aeradio Limited) while others opted to engage their own staff. Now NATS's status in this field is being eroded further with a proposal by the privatised BAA to dispense with the CAA's services at some airports and take over their own visual control rooms. This threat, reported in the CAA's house journal *Airway,* under 'BAA's approach unwelcome', has brought CAA management and unions together in a strange form of shotgun marriage to attempt to fend-off the new broom's attacks on its previously unchallenged and comfortable security.

Shortly after this announcement, although not directly related, the CAA Board decided to transfer some of the air traffic regulatory functions from NATS to the CAA Safety Regulation Group, which is the department that handles pilot licensing, aerodrome licensing and most operational aspects of the authority's activities. This may be a sound move, for in the past NATS has been criticised for operating in isolation from other affected sections and the change may lead to improved internal communication. Clearly, though, the move by airports to turn away from NATS and regulate their own affairs has made its mark, confirmed by a statement from Edge Green, who will head the new Air Traffic Services Standards Department. He says 'With many airfields buying their own equipment and providing their own ATC services, it is necessary to rationalise the regulatory functions to ensure that whoever is providing the service the rules are the same for everybody'. In fact, the causes for concern extend in many other directions, for the Aerodrome Owners Association has expressed worry about the failure of NATS to recognise the ability of other air traffic agencies to handle their own affairs.

As a change from cross-fire between the BAA and the CAA, let us look now at the way in which the airlines and airports fail to live with each other, starting with a cross-Atlantic disagreement about services to and from Manchester. In *The Times* for 30th April 1988 we read:

Attempts to end an Anglo-American squabble over future air services from Manchester to the United States have ended in failure, with both sides refusing to budge and a growing conflict over statistics and long-term US intentions. At the heart of the dispute, which Government officials tried unsuccessfully to tackle in Washington this week, is whether three US airlines should be allowed to begin direct services from Manchester to New York and Boston, when British Airways claims the routes will not even support one British carrier – at least in the short term.

The American carriers, North-West, Pan Am and American airlines are convinced they will be able to fill their aircraft with passengers from throughout the US who are 'fed' into the main hub airports of Chicago, Boston and New York . . .

Manchester airport, which is owned by 10 local authorities, says it does not care who provides the services so long as travellers from the North of England do not have to fly to the congested south-east for their transatlantic flights. It is urging the Government to allow the Americans in . . .

Nearer home, we hear frequent disputes between airline and airline. Almost always the tales are based on jealousies about which company has been awarded a route for a scheduled service. When British Caledonian ceased trading as an independent entity, its routes were not transferred automatically to British Airways, its purchaser, so four airlines applied for the B-Cal route between Gatwick and Nice. The CAA awarded this to Dan Air, but British Island Airways appealed against the authority's decision and Peter Villa, BIA Chaiman, said 'The CAA summed up their verdict by stating that Dan Air's application was "on the face of it . . . more appropriate": hardly the way to justify such an important decision . . .' I offer this not as a criticism of any airline, but to show an example of yet another line among the disagreements that are so rife in the air transport operating industry.

My final quote in this section shows inter-company rivalry at its worst; however, this time is is not the organisations themselves but their employees who reveal their true selves. On 6th May 1988 *The Daily Telegragh* carried a headline 'BROKEN LEGS THREAT TO B-CAL PILOT TRAINERS' with a report credited to an ex B-Cal captain who said 'Far from being the efficient organisation that British Airways propaganda has led us to believe, they have been nothing more than a bunch of amateurs. The number of cancelled flights is beyond belief'. He continued by stating that B-Cal training staff had received letters threatening that any B-Cal training captain who failed a BA pilot would 'have his legs broken and his car smashed.' Did someone say that these were *professional* pilots?

A section on disputes and disagreements would be sadly incomplete without reference to controllers and, of course, their vociferous trade union. Again I could write pages from a combination of personal experiences and press reports, but I will aim to pass the message in brief terms. Broadly, there has been continual argument about whether the controllers are overworked, operating inadequate equipment, underpaid and all the traditional trappings of the union system. To be able to appreciate two sides of the story, however, I include relevant extracts from two reports, from *The Times* (27th April 1988) and *The Independent* (16th August 1988) respectively:

> Allegedly overworked air traffic controllers are taking second jobs ranging from taxi driving to being pilots, MPs were told last night. Mr Christopher Tugendhat, Chairman of the Civil Aviation Authority, told the House of Commons Select Committee on Transport that one controller had a job as a disc jockey, and another as a steel erector; and that he recently received requests for written references for two controllers who had applied to become security guards.
>
> 'Second jobs are a concern to us because there is an inconsistency between claims that people are worked to death and so tired that they cannot work properly and yet they go off to do a second job,' he told the Committee.

The meeting was told that a controller on shift work could earn £26,350, averaging 34¹/₂ hours a week and with 127 days off in a year. A senior controller could earn more than £30,000 a year. So clearly there was more than adequate free time in which to indulge in 'moonlighting', but there was no requirement to do so on grounds of poor pay.

Now, by contrast, to the second report:

> British air controllers are under constant pressure with no respite from heavy traffic flows, according to the controllers' main union.

'There are no quiet periods any more, just constant peaks of work and no troughs to ease the pressure,' Bill Brett, Secretary of the Institute of Professional Civil Servants said. 'Nobody knows what effect this has on safety; it can only be gauged if pilots or controllers make mistakes that kill people.'

One controller who has little support for his union suggested to me that Mr Brett might care to see for himself the boredom through inactivity on a night watch. 'Yet,' he said 'we get paid just as much for that as we do when we work'. Also I received a letter which read 'I am writing on behalf of the Council of the Civil Service Aviation Association to express my concern over the widely reported comments by The Institution of Professional Civil Servants, on the subject on airmiss reports and air traffic control. I wish to make it clear that the views of the IPCS do not represent those of our members . . . The wide publicity given to those comments, which lacked cogency and professional expertise, could be damaging both to the public image of aviation as well as to Civil Servants. I would be grateful if you would make this view known, as soon as possible, through your representation upon NATMAC'.

This was not wholly relevant to the nature of NATMAC's activities, but I am pleased to give it the wider exposure that is available here. The tussle between the union and the CAA was described in a report in *The Daily Telegraph* with 'Lofty considerations such as the future of Britain's crowded skies are continually invoked. The true issues at stake, however, concern such down-to-earth matters as staff levels, rostering, the length of the working week and pay differentials'. Sharp exchanges flowed for many weeks, including a meeting of IPCS, which only 56 members attended (but claiming to represent the country's 1600 controllers), and passed a vote of no confidence in the then Controller of the CAA's National Air Traffic Services. A little later a news release emerged from the CAA which included '. . . ultimately the responsibility for operational decisions must lie with the management and not with the trade unions'. Here it may be interesting to compare the relative strengths of management power in the UK and in the USA, for on the far side of the Atlantic when controllers became too boisterous the Government sacked them and waited for them to creep back quietly.

There are numerous other examples of the controllers' union airing its views. In *The Times* on 11th May 1988 we read 'Official figures suggesting that airmisses are on the decline were misleading and inaccurate, MPs were told last night . . . Biased reports were being submitted by the National Air Traffic Services to the Joint Airmiss Working Group, which was then held 'as an "independent" smokescreen to cover up deficiencies of which it was never aware' the IPCS said.

The Independent for 26th August 1988 reports:

The Secretary of Britain's major air traffic controllers' union has accused the Civil Aviation Authority of blackmailing the BBC into preventing his appearance on last night's television programme "The Travel Show". Bill Brett of the IPCS said he was "dis-invited" from the BBC 2 programme after the CAA refused to appear with him. 'It makes you wonder what the CAA is frightened of', Mr Brett said.

Karen Blumenfeld, the producer, explained 'The CAA were the most important element of the programme . . .; although they agreed to answer questions from passengers they were not happy to appear with Mr Brett. It's not ideal that the CAA appear only under certain conditions, but they are answerable to the public and Mr Brett is not.'

Next the Guild of Air Traffic Control Officers elevated their pitchforks in their journal *Transmit* (issue 2 of 1988), which first took battle with the *Star* for being critical of controllers (accusing that paper of being sensational) and then diverted the attack to the CAA:

> To a large extent CAA management deserved every cringing, squirming minute they had to face in front of a hostile TV interviewer . . . with such a track record it is not surprising that many ATCOs had no sympathy for CAA management who very quickly found themselves subject to questioning by those investigative journalists. (Read that again: you could wonder *whose* track record was being referred to there!)

One outcome of all this hassle is that in January 1989 the CAA decided to establish a committee to examine possible regulation of working hours for controllers. Already the authority has taken action to tighten the existing rules regarding the duty hours for pilots, so naturally – perhaps for the first time – IPCS has expressed some support for a move made by its members' employers. Another change welcomed by the union is that since 1st April 1989 controllers have had access to a new reporting system, whereby without referring to management they can pass details of incidents directly to the CAA's Safety Data and Analysis Unit.

In addition to the well-worn paths of dispute between the controllers and the CAA, the industry has endured the usual monotony of industrial unrest in other quarters, but here I revert briefly to the tabloids. In June 1988 the *Daily Mirror* claimed to have unearthed, under 'Greedy airlines put lives in peril' that young pilots were flying when they were tired, working excessive hours leading to danger. Predictably the paper was egged-on by both the British Airline Pilots Association (BALPA) and the TUC. Shortly before this, on 25th May, the *Daily Express* reported, with a heading 'BA PILOTS POISED TO WORSEN CHAOS', 'Pilots of British Airways will decide tomorrow on a call for industrial action over pay which would greatly increase holiday flight chaos'. Within the industry the cause was clear: that before the BA/B-Cal merger the pilots of the independent company were paid more than their colleagues on the national airline, but the protesters, with BALPA support, had overlooked the hard fact that B-Cal had 'gone under'. Then, more recently, in January 1989, we suffered the threats from airport fire officers (IPCS again) who sought pay increases of 20 per cent. I happened to be aboard a CAA office when this was a warm topic and I overheard a press caller blaming the CAA and then asking what the RAF was doing about it, despite the fact that the men concerned are employed by the privatised BAA!

The industry is far from healthy. Time, thought and energy could and should be concentrated on discovering where the real problems lie and then seeking solutions. Instead, each body operates in isolation, finding great ease and some ill-founded satisfaction in throwing the blame onto another party and then waiting for it to be fired back. This reflects gross lack of both competence and confidence among the people who have been entrusted with positions of responsibility: responsibility, they should be reminded, not to themselves or just to each other, but to a nation that awaits some positive, reasoned action.

This chapter 'Whose is the problem?' needs an answer, but firstly we need to ask '*What* is the problem?' or '*Who* is the problem?' Although constant references to crowded airspace and inadequate runway capacities make comfortable subjects for sparring matches, facts and figures in Chapter 12 prove that both our air and our airports are under-used. If we are incapable of accepting more traffic in the existing-UK system, including the south-east, then it is the people admitting our inabilities who should be in the front line for firing.

Civil aviation must put its act in order and *then* if any real problems remain they can be tackled. An example could be set by the CAA and BAA forming a joint 'achievement council', for until they agree to agree on something sensible we must not be surprised if all the other elements continue to operate independently. There will be problems, of course, because someone will need to concede chairmanship of that body to a rival, but this is where a person's true size may be measured. Those of us who care for the future of British civil aviation await that essential initiative.

Chapter 14
Traffic
Forecasts & Proposals

ALTHOUGH we have established that the present airspace system has more than adequate capacity to absorb the existing and forseeable levels of traffic, we would be unwise to sit back and look no further. A main problem, though, is to find any relevant information that is reliable. Past predictions of demand have failed to match reality and already the revised forecasts published recently by the CAA have been the subject of some criticism; but this is not surprising, for in the world of motorways, in which there is considerably more experience in the task, the errors have proved to be disastrous. All who drive in the south will know the short-comings of the M25 circumventing London, for the jams cannot be missed, but the results in the north have been no more accurate – in the opposite way and therefore not so noticeable. On false forecasts, design standards were hopelessly miscalculated and many millions of pounds were spent on building roads with capacities far in excess of demand, usually dual carriageways with three lanes each way, when two lanes would have been more than sufficient. Although regulated airspace – unlike motorways and airport runways – is not set physically in concrete, the tendency is to take more than is required and to keep it; experience has revealed a marked reluctance to adjust the layout subsequently to suit the proven needs of the time.

Already the airspace planners have ignored advice offered to them in relation to the south-east part of the London Terminal Area. Unlike the fragmented air transport sector, described in the previous chapter, general aviation took the situation sufficiently seriously to unite its strength and present a combined case to the NATS Director of Control (Airspace Policy). Clearly the proposals prepared by NATS would increase the collision risk for by far the majority of airspace users and GA felt that it had a duty to present its own form of rebuttal, so, reluctantly, on 10th January 1989 the Director faced a delegation of twelve representatives to hear the words of warning. As a result of commercial and other pressures, however, he and his colleagues chose to go ahead on the principle of the original plans. Collectively and through individual associations the GA movement felt forced to dissociate itself from the proposed changes and made clear pronouncements to this effect. Decisions based on political rather than safety considerations cannot be accepted as recipes for long-term success.

To give users even less confidence in the planning system, the change to the LTMA conflicts with NATS' own stated policy published in the glossy hand-out known as NATS Operational Strategy Plan, dated as recently as September 1988 and quoted in Chapter 4. In the document, on page 27, we read: 'In the past . . . [planning philosophy] . . . has been manifested in a segregation of airspace to separate the different activities; for the future greater emphasis will be placed on the sharing of airspace to the mutual benefit of all users. The possibilities include . . . . [re controlled airspace] . . . . reductions in the hours of its use.' Two pages ahead we find 'New designs and improvements in airborne and ground equipment will lead to reductions of current separation standards and thus to increases in the capacity of airspace'. Perhaps we may need to wait for a year or two before the second point can be applied, but the first proposal was published only four months before NATS chose to ignore its own promises and enforce even greater segregation than had applied before the change. At the time of going to press, no reason has been offered; but perhaps none can be found?

I mention this here because many people live with the fear that despite the strategy statements NATS will over-react to the traffic forecasts and produce some even more potentially damaging proposals. The alleged upsurge in holiday traffic in 1988, used as an excuse to justify the chaos, turned out to be a very small increase (and in the case of many operators a reduction) and the demand for 1989 has shown a marked decrease. So where do we find the justification for a projection showing a rise almost to infinity? The motorway planners were guilty of this and received some rough rides at public inquiries, but the CAA is relatively inexperienced in the field of forecasting and may well be unaware of all that has gone before. Those who wish to see benefit from predicting endless expansion of travel demand can do so by a blind, almost naïve, belief in a constant economic growth, which has not happened yet and is very unlikely to do so in the coming years. Yet on 2nd February 1989 the authority issued a lengthy tome 'Traffic Distribution Policy for the London Area and Strategic Options for the Long Term' (CAP 548), which states that by 2005 the number of passengers at London's four airports will have more than doubled to 123 million. These figures relate to Heathrow, Gatwick, Luton and Stansted; London City appears to play no significant part in these anticipated growths. The forecast levels for the year 2000, given with the 1988 figures for comparison, are as follows for the chief airports in south-east England:

	1988	2000
Heathrow	38m	49m
Gatwick	22m	30m
Luton	2.7m	5m
Stansted	1.1m	16.5m
Bournemouth	0.16m	2m
Southend	0.16m	0.75m
Southampton	0.4m	1.5m
Manston	0.01m	5m
Lydd	Nil	0.3m

Among the points mentioned in the consultative document are confirmation that no additional measures to affect traffic distribution need to be taken until 1995; but, by then, lack of airport (rather than airspace) capacity in the London area will cause considerable extensions in activity at some regional airports, although projecting further ahead to 2005 it is possible that Stansted could be handling up to 60 per cent of London's long-haul traffic; for this, though, an additional runway and new terminals would be needed. Passengers travelling through Heathrow or Gatwick can expect to pay substantially higher costs and some will be priced out of travelling by air, although the document tends to be self-contradicting by stating that charter traffic should not be forced away from Gatwick by giving priority to scheduled services.

The acquisition of larger aircraft is expected to enable airports and the airspace system to handle more passengers with fewer movements; but how many times have we heard this?

The policy document contains several other points to note, including for the first time an admission that forecasting demand is very difficult, confessing the fallibility of past predictions. Also, following an earlier prompting from within the GA movement, the CAA admits, also for the first time, that the opening of the Channel Tunnel will have a considerable effect on air traffic demand. It considers a likely reduction from the rising trend of 5 million passengers and 50,000 movements in 1995 and 6 million passengers and 60,000 movements by 2000. Not to be outdone by another travel mode, however, the CAA claims that if the forecasts for the effects of the Channel Tunnel are over optimistic and air traffic is not diverted to the extent predicted, then for a few years the London airspace system would face very severe constraints.

Many points of relevance have been confused or overlooked in the assessment of the situation ahead. There is, for instance, reference to the need for a second runway at Stansted, whereas only a few months have passed since the industry named either Bournemouth or Kent International as the most likely place for physical expansion. No-one has been bold enough to suggest that additional runway capacity is needed both to the north and to the south of London and this aspect will be watched very closely to prevent such thoughts being allowed to develop by stealth. Perhaps this is not really intended; it may be no more ominous than a failure of communication between the left and the right hands of authority. Indeed the matter of runways poses a further question, for only a few weeks before the publication of CAP 548 (which must have been at the printers by then) Paul Channon, Secretary of State for Transport, announced (*The Independent*, 21st December 1988) that new runways for the London area were not yet on the agenda.

The frequently conflicting information that emerges from a range of official sources weakens the case for placing any trust in the traffic forecasts, which bear little relation to current trends in the demands for the movement of people. Also, the suggestion in CAP 548 that the forecasts for the effect of the Channel Tunnel may be too optimistic reflects once again a failure by the CAA to study transport developments in a wider context. The tunnel may be a key link in the proposed expansion of the European rail system, but it is only one part of the plan. As with all predictions, it is possible that the full scope of the project involving 14 nations may not be realised, but part of it is under way already. Here France takes the lead, with routes already under construction for running 190 mph trains throughout the country and, to prove the point, already a *train-à-grande-vitesse* (TGV) has achieved a record speed of 254 mph. The total plan envisages a network of nearly 19,000 miles of high-speed track stretching from Edinburgh to Madrid, Lisbon and Athens; and already at this very early stage 14 per cent of the TGV custom has been creamed from the airlines. So while most realists agree that the tunnel will take a very substantial percentage of the passengers now travelling by air on short routes such as those between London and Paris or Brussels, the

first phase of the rail development scheme will link London not only with both those towns but also with Amsterdam, Cologne and Frankfurt. The rail promoters are confident that the travel times between these centres will be halved, so most of the air routes to and from Europe may suffer downgrades in demand to match those of our existing internal air services. All this heralds some very serious competition for short-haul airlines, which makes existing traffic forecasting figures even less meaningful.

As a contrast, even though Charles de Gaulle Airport near Paris is expected to oust Heathrow as Europe's main air link with the USA, the longer routes may develop more fully; so if there is an overall increase in movements in the London area, one new scheme, known as the Central Control Function (CCF), will absorb this easily by adding between 30 per cent and 40 per cent to the existing airspace capacity in the south-east. Basically this divides the airspace into discrete blocks, so that traffic outbound from Heathrow will use its own 'tunnels' and traffic inbound to Stansted will use others, with each major airport having its own separate arrival and departure tubes.

The main advantage of this concept is that each tunnel has a one-way flow with all aircraft travelling in the same direction. In normal circumstances one controller will be responsible for a complete tunnel, handling each aircraft almost from its arrival in UK airspace until it reaches its destination airport. At present, when one aircraft reaches the edge of a sector, it is handed over to the next controller and the process needs to be repeated several times. This involves considerable co-ordination and, with the world's best will, opens the doors for potential error in the hand-over process.

CCF will remove the need for most of this co-ordination, easing the controller's task and increasing the number of aircraft which the existing airspace system can handle. Each block of air will be separate from each adjacent tunnel by at least three nautical miles horizontally and 1000 feet vertically. Apart from the scheme's ability to handle a very substantial traffic increase in relation to the amount of airspace required, it should enable controllers to reduce or even eliminate the need for queuing in 'stacks', which cause so much delay today. In reverse, departing aircraft will be cleared to attain their optimum cruising levels more rapidly.

Each airport has its own visual control room to handle take-offs and the final stages of arrivals (which clearly must be retained) but also each has its own approach control to handle traffic in the surrounding airspace. However, CCF will centralise this facility, with Heathrow, Gatwick and Stansted approach functions absorbed into the London Air Traffic Control Centre (LATCC) at West Drayton.

The Central Control Function will be phased in over five years from a start in 1990 and when the system is fully operational all criss-crossing of commercial air traffic will cease. Perhaps this is the most significant single development in air traffic control since the introduction of radar, but already some cynics have aired their views. Firstly, the idea is not new and is not the brain-child of a genius within NATS, but is copied from a system that has operated successfully for several years around New York. Why, some ask, was it not introduced in the UK sooner? The cost at about £30 million is not prohibitive by national expenditure standards and is a fraction of the figure spent on other ATC projects, which are scheduled to require a total investment of more than £600 million; recently-installed UK *en route* radars alone have cost £50 million. I am assured that the 'know-how' for CCF has been available for more than ten years and the cost is not a deterrent, so if the initiative had been grabbed more speedily all the

Air traffic controllers assisting with development of the Central Control Function and using prototypes of the new vertical control suites. (Courtesy CAA)

irritation caused by earlier delays could have been avoided and the word 'airspace' might have escaped the tabloid vocabulary. When it is fully operational, though, the Central Control Function will be a vast improvement on any methods that have been used so far. This will enhance not only the speed of handling, but will remove the potential traffic conflicts caused by sector hand-overs, so safety, too, will improve.

This leads us to LATCC itself which came into being as such in 1971. It is responsible for air traffic services in not only the immediate London area, but extends through England to latitude 55° north and includes the Isle of Man, Wales and Northern Ireland, together with the surrounding areas until they meet airspace that is under the operational care of other countries. There is a sub-centre at Manchester which handles traffic below 15,000 feet in that area. Also LATCC provides a Flight Information Service as a facility for aircraft flying outside controlled airspace, but this safety service has been reduced recently, allegedly due to a shortage of available controllers. Apart from the needs of civil users, LATCC incorporates a Military Area Services Operations Room and London Military Radar Services, to provide guidance for aircraft operated by British and overseas forces in the airspace within the Centre's jurisdiction. Shortly, at a cost of £23 million, the centre will have the benefit of a new IBM comuter.

Just as the operating industry has suffered alternate shortages and surpluses of pilots, the air traffic management has been no better in knowing its needs. In 1985 there were ructions in the ranks of controllers, for NATS planned some extensive redundancies, but these failed to occur and within two years the system began to suffer because there were too few qualified people to staff the posts. In 1987 only

30 trainees were enrolled into the College of Air Traffic Control at Bournemouth; 80 were admitted in the following year and for 1989 the figure is 140. From 1990 onward the proposed intake will be 180 a year. Many people in the aviation industry find considerable difficuly in accepting these as valid requirements, for the introduction of the CCF alone will reduce the number of people needed and already the staff strength at LATCC is more than double the number of commercial air transport aircraft on the UK register. At least one Member of Parliament – rightly or otherwise – has been looking closely at this and is awaiting developments.

Another area of proposed change concerns the methods by which CAT aircraft (and many others) can be brought safely onto runways for landing. When in the air, pilots use various fixed navigation aids, with VHF Omni-directional Ranges (VOR), Distance Measuring Equipment (DME) and Non-Directional Beacons (NDB) at almost 100 sites throughout the UK. Then there is primary radar, which shows a machine's position on the ground-based screen in relation to the radar head (the site) and secondary surveillance radar (SSR) which relies on a transponder aboard the aeroplane to return the signal in the form of convertible information, including the callsign and operational data such as the destination. All this procedure is firmly established in the operating system, but strong pressures are at work to replace the well-known, well-tried and wholly successful Instrument Landing System (ILS) by a less proven microwave landing system (MLS). Predictably, there is marked resistance among airlines and airports to this change and the only reason that anyone has put forward in its favour is that the VHF frequency band used for ILS localiser beams cannot be given guaranteed protection from interference in the long term. Despite this, in 1988, new ILS installations were completed at Heathrow, where the General Manager of Air Traffic Services described it (*Skypost*, 2nd June 1988) with 'the end product is that we have the most modern and reliable ILS available in the world'. At higher level, Sir John Charnley, who is Chairman of the CAA's Research and Development Programme Board stated (*Computer World* for April/May 1988) 'hard evidence and facts about MLS are singularly lacking . . . . in an ILS environment, airport and airline operators could see no benefits offered by MLS'.

Yet although so far no-one has offered any positive advantages that the new MLS system is likely to offer, the scheme blunders ahead. Certainly it will not improve safety for anyone, it will cost considerable sums to airports for ground equipment and to operators for airborne sets and in the latter case I have heard one airline ask how space is to be found in aircraft that already are crammed with essential items. Before you suggest that the new MLS will replace the existing ILS, the two systems will be running together for several years, because not all airports will re-equip at the same time; on present schedules, apart from trial installations, proposed MLS introduction years range from 1991 for Heathrow's runway 09L to 2000 for Cardiff and Bristol. At the time of going to press, Birmingham is the largest airport to have no plans for installing MLS, but others include Blackpool, Humberside, Plymouth, Southampton and Teesside. So both ILS *and* MLS equipment will be needed aboard many aircraft for several years ahead.

The microwave landing system is being pursued even more energetically by its protagonists in the USA than is the case in this country, but, equally, the resistance there is more strongly united. From the USA AOPA *Pilot* for August 1988 we read 'The Federal Aviation Administration has been criticised for the poor handling of the $17-billion project, one of the most costly in the National

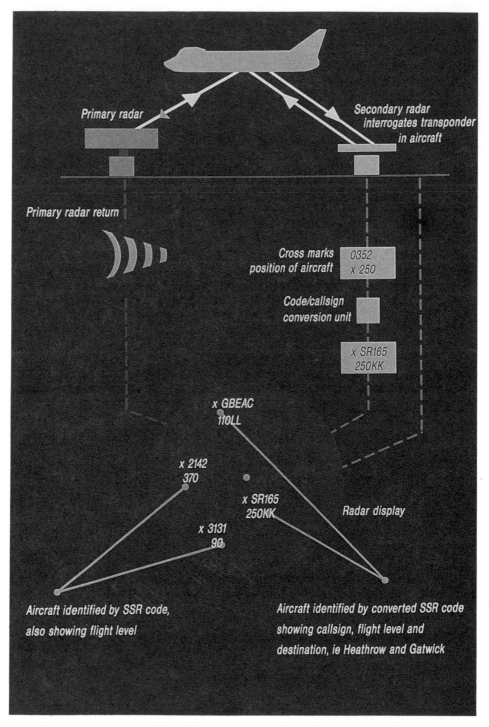

Primary radar

Secondary radar
interrogates transponder
in aircraft

Primary radar return

Cross marks
position of aircraft

0352
x 250

Code/callsign
conversion unit

x SR165
250KK

x GBEAC
110LL

x 2142
370

x SR165
250KK

Radar display

x 3131
90

Aircraft identified by SSR code,
also showing flight level

Aircraft identified by converted SSR code
showing callsign, flight level and
destination, ie Heathrow and Gatwick

A schematic representation of how the two types of radar allow an aircraft's position, height,
126 *destination and identity to be plotted for purposes of air traffic control. (Courtesy CAA)*

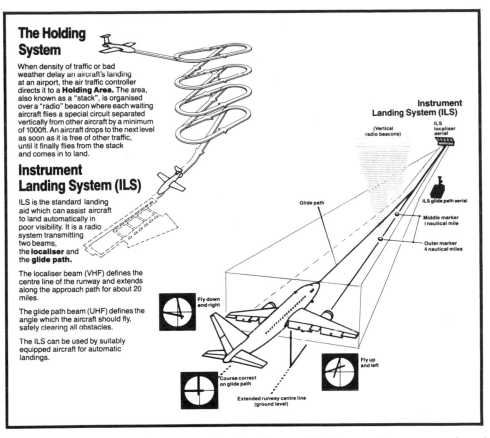

The Holding System

When density of traffic or bad weather delay an aircraft's landing at an airport, the air traffic controller directs it to a **Holding Area.** The area, also known as a "stack", is organised over a "radio" beacon where each waiting aircraft flies a special circuit separated vertically from other aircraft by a minimum of 1000ft. An aircraft drops to the next level as soon as it is free of other traffic, until it finally flies from the stack and comes in to land.

Instrument Landing System (ILS)

ILS is the standard landing aid which can assist aircraft to land automatically in poor visibility. It is a radio system transmitting two beams, the **localiser** and the **glide path.**

The localiser beam (VHF) defines the centre line of the runway and extends along the approach path for about 20 miles.

The glide path beam (UHF) defines the angle which the aircraft should fly, safely clearing all obstacles.

The ILS can be used by suitably equipped aircraft for automatic landings.

Instrument Landing System (ILS)

(Vertical radio beacons)

ILS localiser aerial

Glide path

ILS glide path aerial

Middle marker I nautical mile

Outer marker 4 nautical miles

Fly down and right

Fly up and left

Course correct on glide path

Extended runway centre line (ground level)

How an aircraft uses an Instrument Landing System (ILS) to make an approach and landing at an airfield. (Courtesy CAA)

Airspace System plan. The MLS project is 30 months behind schedule and its benefits over the existing ILS have yet to be proven'. The US General Accounting Office, a federal watchdog agency, has released a study of the MLS programme called 'MLS: Additional Systems Should Not Be Procured Unless Benefits Proven' which includes 'the FAA has not adequately demonstrated the benefits, nor addressed safety and reliability questions of using MLS in challenging operational environments'. While the disagreements over MLS continue, within the past year one company in the USA has obtained firm contracts for 17 new ILS installations and has options for a further 42!

You may wonder why I have devoted so much space to reports about equipment that will have little influence on safety and almost certainly will not offer any improvements. I feel that I have a good reason, for finance is finite and any funds that are available should be geared and steered to projects that will be of benefit to as many organisations and people as possible; not just to those who are selling the system.

On a happier note, already I have mentioned the new *en route* radars. Six of these have been introduced to service over a period of eight years and the final installation was commissioned in October 1988. This was at the remote Great Dun Fell in the North Pennines. These new primary and secondary surveillance

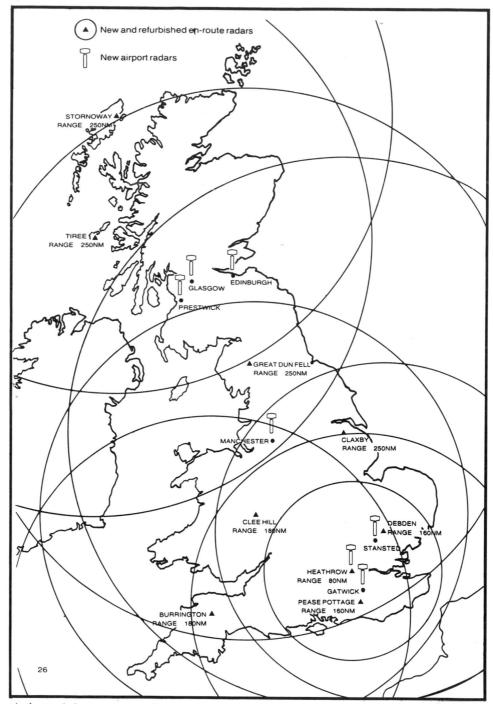

A chart of the positions and coverage of airport and en route *radars in the UK. (Courtesy CAA)*

radars provide the UK with greatly enhanced coverage and they help both to improve safety and to enable more aircraft to use the available airspace. They operate in conjunction with earlier stations and they are fully compatible with the older existing equipment. As the operation is monitored and controlled from LATCC the sites are mainly unmanned. Also new local radar installations are in the process of being provided at nine UK airports, at a collective cost of £11 million.

Among other developments in the safety line are traffic alert and collision avoidance systems (TCAS). Here the USA is taking the lead by not only instructing US airlines operating aircraft with more than 30 seats to be equipped by December 1991, but requiring other countries' carriers operating in US airspace to be similarly fitted. Almost certainly there is no possibility of operators meeting this deadline, which has been created by the FAA following political pressures from Congress, and no doubt some compromise will be reached. Although preliminary trials are under way in Britain, where the Royal Aerospace Establishment (RAE) is using a Boeing 737 on loan from British Airways with a British Aerospace 125 serving as the 'target' aircraft, ICAO has not agreed an international standard and this may lead to problems when traffic is transferred from one nation's airspace to that controlled by a different country.

Basically TCAS involves the use of air-traffic transponders and when one machine approaches another it instructs a pilot to climb or descend to avoid a collision; eventually a version known as TCAS III will have the added capacity to order pilots to turn left or right. So far, though, the CAA has remained reasonably cool about the operational use of this equipment, for although when fully developed it will improve safety, at present there is a fear that the system may generate too many spurious readings for effective and reliable use; but clearly it will come and then it will be a safety bonus to be welcomed. One source states that the likely cost of the airborne equipment will be in the region of £100,000 for each aircraft. Spread over the remaining life of an airframe this may be a minor expense in the list of moves designed to improve safety, but each additional feature adds to the carrier's costs, so passengers must be prepared to pay more for their seats to enjoy the added security that new developments will offer.

Looking further ahead there are world wide plans for replacing existing navigation methods by the use of satellites. ICAO has studied the possibilities in detail through the Special Committee on Future Air Navigation Systems (FANS) and here I quote a few extracts from the Organisation's bulletin:

Those satellite navigation systems that are planned or are being studied are capable of providing an accuracy of some tens of metres at any point on the globe. The advantages of such systems are very attractive for civil aviation users.

Aircraft equipment is universal since it can operate everywhere (oceans, polar or desert areas, mountainous regions etc) and thereby relieve operators of the need to mount multiple navigation systems on board aircraft; and they enable non-precision approaches to be made to runways that are not otherwise equipped. . . .

In the longer term, satellite navigation systems could replace all conventional radio navigation systems, which would enable the ground infrastructures to be abandoned. . . .

The GPS – NavStar system, which is the best documented one today and seems to be the most advanced, should be operational in the early 1990s. . . makes it a highly attractive candidate for civil aviation because of the expected 100-metre accuracy.

. . . It should also be specified that complexity no longer necessarily implies high prices and that amortizing the main developments will be allowed for in military equipment.

In case the last statement generates a feeling of fear in the mind of the reader because of the likelihood of trouble from an unfriendly nation, this extract from the same document may eliminate that concern:

Though this system is designed for all mobile user groups, it especially meets the requirements of civil aviation. Moreover, due to its centralised structure, no state could interfere with reliable operation of the system. Thus, it is well suited to be operated and controlled by an international agency.

Although technical advances are being made very rapidly, this promising development, which will greatly increase the accuracy of air navigation and therefore add a further improvement to safety, will reach practical fruition only if the will exists in places of power. I quote from a report by Jan Smit, Chairman of FANS, published in *The Journal of Air Traffic Control* (published by the International Federation of Air Traffic Controllers Associations) no. 3 of 1988:

Members of the Council and of the Air Navigation Commission must carry the urgent message to their Governments; every Director of Civil Aviation or equivalent and other leaders in the aviation industry at large, including user organisations, must ensure that the required priorities are established . . . . Unless these steps are taken, and urgently, the excellent proposal of the FANS Committee may never be realised and eventually civil aviation will bear the consequences.

The FANS Committee concluded that satellite-based communication, navigation and surveillance systems will be the key to improvements of the air navigation environment on a global scale . . . . The fate of the proposal is now in the hands of the national Civil Aviation Administrations throughout the world. What importance do they attach to civil aviation's control of its technical destiny, with all the related effects on the safety, regularity and efficiency of civil aviation operations?

The work that led to this stage began in 1983, when FANS was formed; now it is operating with membership from 22 contracting states within ICAO. The benefits to all branches of aviation are almost endless, for the enormous increase in the accuracy of navigation will enable far more aircraft to operate in greater safety and in far less airspace, which in turn will release substantial areas for other users. We must remember that the CAT sector is not the only growth story, for GA is expanding at a faster rate and satellite navigation will help to ensure that there is a relative freedom in the supply of space for all users. The present airways routes will be redundant and most regulated airspace will be surplus to need.

The final point for this chapter is nearer in terms of both time and distance: European liaison. There has been a long and – until recently – understandable tendency for each nation to fly its own flag and to operate without much consideration for its neighbour's needs. During the past few years, however, moves have started to co-ordinate airspace activities on a centralised basis throughout Europe.

The Eurocontrol Convention was established as long ago as 1st March 1963, with eight states currently in membership and two more on the brink of joining. Most of the policy papers that have emerged so far fall short of positive action and a fact sheet produced in July 1988 by the UK Department of Transport stressed nine points: only one was new. Most of these were shadows of matters that had been planned five or more years previously by the ICAO European Civil Aviation Conference (ECAC). Several instances of leadership claimed from British sources have been matched by a roughly equal supply of critical condemnation from others. I quote a few:

> Britain called yesterday for a European-wide air traffic centre to deal with the summer congestion and delays which plague the continent's airways. Paul Channon, the Secretary of State for Transport, yesterday proposed a new flow management centre at Maastricht in Holland to co-ordinate the rates at which aircraft take-off and land across Europe. It would be run by Eurocontrol, the eight-nation agency for air navigation safety . . . . The real question is whether there is the political will in Europe?

For this information we are indebted to *The Independent* dated 28 September 1988.

At about the same time Keith Mack, then Controller, National Air Traffic Services commented (*Airway*, October 1988):

> We have been seeking European co-operation and co-ordination for some time. This is a vital step in alleviating the problems experienced during the summer and the Secretary of State's initiative is most welcome.

About two months later a statement from the Netherlands by the Vice-President of the Eurocontrol Guild of Air Traffic Services included:

> Eurocontrol has not yet become the European organisation that was envisaged simply because of a lack of political will, and not because of a lack of willingness or capability on the part of the Eurocontrol organisation.

Since then, Mr Mack has become Director-General of Eurocontrol and we await developments, but he may have a problem. Read now this extract from a 1988 European Parliament Briefing under 'Air Traffic Control – a European or a national responsibility?'

> Deregulation has led to an increase in air traffic but more and more flights are delayed as air traffic controllers work around the clock trying to cope with Europe's congested air space. This has led to further concerns about safety.
>
> Petrus Cornelissen (N.EPP) reporting for the transport committee, considers the best way round the problem would be to co-ordinate national control centres through a Western European umbrella organisation modelled on the US Federal Aviation Administration, which is responsible for the whole of US airspace.
>
> Eurocontrol (European organisation for the safety of air navigation) would seem to be in an ideal position to take on this role, but as Mr Cornelissen points

out, its competence has been significantly undermined by national authorities since its foundation in 1960 (*sic*). *France and the UK refused to concede any air traffic control duties to the European agency*, based at Maastricht, and in 1985 Belgium decided to set up a new national air traffic control centre, thus limiting the effectiveness of Eurocontrol even further. . . .

. . . At the same time Mr Cornelissen would like to see increased co-operation between the military and civil aviation authorities, since at present certain air corridors are reserved exclusively for military aircraft. For example a civilian flight from Manchester to Brussels is not allowed to pass over East Anglia and must instead go via London's already overcrowded airspace.

The italics are mine and the message is clear.

Also from the continent, we hear this from the secretary-general of the Association of European Airlines: 'What is needed urgently is increased investment in airport and air traffic control, but even this will not be enough without a co-ordinated European approach to ATC'.

Such remarks are heard not only in mainland Europe, for here I quote from our own lower House. *Hansard* for 26th July 1988 reads:

My Right Honourable friend the Secretary of State must ensure that the directors of each international air traffic control system have their heads collectively banged together until there is a unified system all over Europe.

So this is how we stand at a point well into 1989. The recent record in the decision-making process is not one that inspires high levels of confidence in those entrusted with the planning tasks that lie ahead; but I am sure that most readers will join me in hoping that a new wave of competence in both direction and management will appear and, belatedly, the business of steering civil aviation into the nineties and beyond will be taken as seriously as today's situation demands.

Pertinent postcript

Already the CAA's predictions for almost endless growth in traffic demand have been shattered to a level of fantasy, with 585,000 fewer reservations for fun-in-the-sun flights in 1989 compared with the previous year. Also, more recently, BAA airports collectively recorded a reduction of 10.4 per cent in short-haul charter traffic in each of the first two months of the 1989 holiday season compared with the same months of 1988. These recent decreases are greater than the increases that were used as excuses for the chaos then, so over the past two years we have had a net reduction in such bookings. These figures leave little justification – unless we are prepared to accept gross mishandling of existing resources as being justifiable – for any runway, airport or airspace congestion.

Chapter 15
Outlook Unsettled

A BOOK with a title that poses a question must provide an answer and, as this is the final chapter, I cannot delay that task for much longer. If, however, the solution could be in the form of a straight yes/no verdict, I would not have written all this and you would not have needed to wade your way through it.

When I decided to unite pen with paper to produce some findings on the safety of UK airspace, I had hoped to be able to trace sound reasons to explain some of the strange practices with which civil aviation has been smitten; but I was not so fortunate. The more that I assembled my own findings and the further I delved into the discoveries of others, the picture developed progressively as one that needed to be exposed in a way that I had not intended at the start.

Sometimes the truth is not easy to digest. Many people will not like what they – and even less will they like what others – read about their performances, for the overall scene is not one of a well directed and efficiently managed industry. At various points in the text I have mentioned the incredible levels of disagreement that have been allowed to continue when there is an urgent need for constructive thinking and positive action. I am not seeking to cause personal embarrassment and I will not repeat any detail from the earlier chapters, but in fairness to some people I must pin-point a little more precisely some sources of error.

The long-range arguments between the BAA and the CAA reflect discredit on both bodies and certainly they have achieved nothing in the search for solutions. The fact that politicians, the press and the public have singled the CAA as the most regular target may not be surprising, but here I intend to surprise you by being kind. The term 'CAA' has been used in a broad-brush sense and I have counted the examples of criticism that have been aimed at the Authority. Roughly six out of every seven attacks on file have been intended for National Air Traffic Services and it is unfair that the other sections should be brought into the shooting line for blame. Certainly no department is wholly free from accusation, but, by virtue of its constitution, NATS has almost escaped public mention by name and it is right that here it should be brought into the open and placed on the counting line.

Let me divert now, from the people who share the task of finding ways to provide the holidaymakers with their desires, to those who do the seeking. So far, I have not said much about their seemingly endless expectations, but now I quote from a thoughtful editorial in *The Independent* that appeared in the midst of the summer shambles of 1988, on 18th July:

A blight brought home to Blighty

There is something Malthusian in the way in which mass tourism is choking in its own excesses. At its worst, it is a form of blight, killing the thing it loves. Now, after ravaging many a Mediterranean town, village, beach and even whole coastlines, the blight has come back to strike at its own sources in northern Europe. The annual flight to the south has been checked at the starting post. There is some rough justice in this. If tourism pollutes, the polluter – innocent as an individual but guilty *en masse* – is now paying the price.

To point the finger of blame solely at the Civil Aviation Authority is to indulge in the British taste for scapegoats . . . the reckless over-scheduling of British charter operators who attempt to pack too many trips into too few hours.

. . . Technical solutions, tighter controls and even perhaps a quota system for north-south air traffic might make Europe's skies less crowded and less dangerous. But best of all would be a more thinking approach by travellers and the tourist industry alike. When northern as well as southern Europe has so much to offer, the painful airborne odyssey to crowded Mediterranean beaches makes less and less sense.

So here we have another angle. The finger of blame is directed not at the CAA (no, not even NATS), nor the BAA, nor the controllers or their union. It is aimed at you.

Still another aspect, mentioned lightly in an earlier chapter, is the factor that is most likely to curtail future holiday flights. From *Flight International* for 10th December 1988 I quote the final part of the main editorial:

The limit on air transport growth might prove not to be airspace, airports, or aircraft, but pilots. To service growth so far, airlines have engaged in a form of feeding chain: majors recruit from regionals, regionals from general aviation, and GA from the private flying community.

Already flying clubs report a severe shortage of instructors, raising fears that the pool of self-starter pilots could dry up before airlines have had time to establish *ab initio* training programmes on the scale required.

The potential impact on safety of over-stretching any sector of the air transport industry is so great that it deserves the closest attention from all those in a position to influence the industry over the coming years.

Note that safety plays key roles in both these editorial extracts. Also, from the *Flight* leader, that the private and club flying movement is the essential nest-box for the survival of commercial air transport as a species; for whatever pilot training schemes are financed by the airlines, there is no possibility that these will fulfil the needs of all operators.

We are nearly there. My aim is neither to blame not to appease, but as the future of British aviation safety is so important, I have needed to push against a few doors that normally are kept firmly closed. For some, truth is not only hard to accept, but for that same reason it is hard to find. I place high value on truth's merits, however, and the points that have been unearthed in this book must be

addressed by those who are paid to oversee the workings of the system. Success will demand more open thinking than we have seen so far and parochial interests must be pushed into the bin of history. Whether the current incumbents are able to match and master the task is one that we all wait to see. The Challenge – and therefore the chance – exist now.

Safety for the future, therefore, depends on many things, but on a relatively few people. To retain our freedom and our way of life we must have space for military aviation; for reasons just mentioned – and for others explained earlier – we depend on a healthy general aviation movement; and if people are to have happy holidays we require a viable and efficient commercial air transport sector. By world standards our sky is relatively empty and there is adequate space for all, but this must be established and agreed on a mutual-need basis and not forced into shape by external pressures that are not geared to the main aim; in short, people's lives must have priority over politics.

Now to a verdict. Perhaps it is superfluous to remind you of the disarray in which aviation seems to survive, but despite that, we can deserve some credit. We are concerned here with airspace and what goes on within it, so although an accident *can* occur at any time, remember this: occasionally ships collide and some sink; sometimes trains hit each other; many cars, lorries and their occupants are destroyed every day, but no British-operated civil transport aircraft has hit another machine in the air since 1954 – and even that was outside British airspace and all the people on board escaped unhurt. The only occasion on which an airliner hit another aeroplane whilst flying over Britain was in 1949. By my reckoning, 40 years is a long period of mid-air safety and one for which we can claim some pride – so long as this stops before we reach and accept complacency.

I must repeat that thoughts on safety are wholly subjective and the figures previously quoted confirm without doubt which travel modes are safe and which are not so safe. Yet, when we have an occasional air or rail accident, because of the rarity, still someone shouts to demand some form of action and others express public fears about air or rail travel. This is purely escapism, for we can pass the responsibility onto others, but because we know that the level of safety on the roads is largely in our *own* hands, we accept the likelihood of death (to refresh on this go back to Chapter 3) and ignore the danger with neither fuss nor apparent fear.

The rail accident near Glasgow on 6th March 1989, in which two unfortunate people died, was considered sufficiently newsworthy to appear as the main headline topic in at least six national daily newspapers; the story was accompanied by calls for improved warning and signalling equipment and, of course, greater investment to provide it. Yet nowhere could I find any newspaper reference to the 14 people who were killed on the roads on that same day. A sobering addition to that situation is that if a rail accident similar to the one near Glasgow occurred every week throughout the year, travel by train would be more than six times safer than car travel in the annual statistics. The case in support of air travel safety is broadly comparable.

Aviation's past record is very good. The alarm that has accompanied it is not. There is work ahead to ensure that our airspace remains safe in the future, but there is little point in endeavouring to achieve this without planning for *all* users to have the room that they require in order to conduct their operations. Theoretical safety for one sector by banning another is an unacceptable and dangerous way to solve a problem, for it creates a new and possibly bigger one. Yet, to the south of London that situation exists now and the planners must rectify the errors that they introduced in April 1989. If they fail, the record ahead may not be so clean as the one that we have behind us.

Finally, a quote. I am not sure where this originated, but it was rejuvenated recently when it found its way into a page of *Flight International*, to which I am indebted:

To be completely safe you must sit on a fence and watch the birds . . . but you can be very nearly as safe in the air. Take much comfort from that.